Dwarf Rabbits as a Hobby

by Dennis Kelsey-Wood

SAVE-OUR-PLANET SERIES

T.F.H. Publications, Inc.
1 T.F.H. Plaza • Third & Union Aves. • Neptune, NJ 07753

Contents

Photography: Bruce Crook, Isabelle Français, Michael Gilroy, Ray Hanson, Horst Mayer, Michael Mettler, and David Robinson.

Distributed in the UNITED STATES to the Pet Trade by T.F.H. Publications, Inc., One T.F.H. Plaza, Neptune City, NJ 07753; distributed in the UNITED STATES to the Bookstore and Library Trade by National Book Network, Inc. 4720 Boston Way, Lanham MD 20706; in CANADA to the Pet Trade by H & L Pet Supplies Inc., 27 Kingston Crescent, Kitchener, Ontario N2B 2T6; Rolf C. Hagen Ltd., 3225 Sartelon Street, Montreal 382 Quebec; in CANADA to the Book Trade by Macmillan of Canada (A Division of Canada Publishing Corporation), 164 Commander Boulevard, Agincourt, Ontario M1S 3C7; in ENGLAND by T.F.H. Publications, PO Box 15, Waterlooville PO7 6BQ; in AUSTRALIA AND THE SOUTH PACIFIC by T.F.H. (Australia), Pty. Ltd., Box 149, Brookvale 2100 N.S.W., Australia; in NEW ZEALAND by Brooklands Aquarium Ltd., 5 McGiven Drive, New Plymouth, RD1 New Zealand; in the PHILIPPINES by Bio-Research, 5 Lippay Street, San Lorenzo Village, Makati, Rizal; in SOUTH AFRICA by Multipet Pty. Ltd., P.O. Box 35347, Northway, 4065, South Africa. Published by T.F.H. Publications, Inc. Manufactured in the United States of America by T.F.H. Publications, Inc.

Polish, blue-eyed white. In this book, the author has used the popular view of a dwarf rabbit in determining which breeds should be included. This means that, apart from the breeds that have the word *dwarf* in their names, the Polish, the Britannia Petite, the Jersey Wooly, the Holland (Dwarf) Lop, and the American Fuzzy Lop can all be regarded as dwarfs.

Acknowledgments

In the preparation of any pet-animal book, be it large or small, an author needs to refer to the data and information compiled over the years by those enthusiasts that form the backbone of the respective animal hobby. Without these people and organizations, informative facts simply would not be available. I would like to thank the officers of both the British Rabbit Council and the American Rabbit Breeders Association, Inc. for their constant readiness to supply facts and advice related to rabbits. I would also like to thank the following people who kindly gave advice and information related to specific dwarf rabbit breeds and their history: Ronald Varner (Holland Lop), Dale Isles (Mini Lop), Mary Louise Cowan (Dwarf Hotot), Mona Berryhill (Mini Rex), and Jeff Hardin (Holland and Mini Lops). To Tracey Prins, a special thanks for her diligent work in transposing this author's thousands of jumbled animal facts into a cohesive bank of computer files.

American Fuzzy Lop.

Introduction

All of the domestic rabbits, which adults and children have for centuries loved, bred, and kept within the confines of their homes, are descendants of the European, or Old World, wild rabbit *Oryctolagus cuniculus*. From this agouti-colored species that weighs 3 to 5 lbs. have been developed quite literally hundreds of breeds and varieties. Many of them have now become extinct through lack of popularity or because they were crossed with other breeds and their names changed. However, others have replaced them, so the hobby is always progressing forward. At this time, in the USA and Britain, there are about 65 breeds, and they are seen in a tremendous array of colors and patterns—so many in fact, that a newcomer can be spoiled when making his choice.

BRIEF DOMESTIC HISTORY

It is thought that rabbits were first domesticated in

Jersey Wooly, one of the newer dwarf rabbit breeds. Its pleasing appearance is a combination of the diminutive size of a dwarf rabbit and a profuse wool coat.

Spain, but exactly when is not known. By about 800 B.C., the Phoenicians, who were a major seafaring power at that time, are thought to have obtained rabbit stock from that country and dispersed them as a salable product around the Near East. Later in time, rabbits were popular food items for the Romans, who kept them in walled gardens called *lepororii*. There is no doubt that the Romans aided the spread of rabbits as one of the food items for their legions as they moved across Europe and Asia. It is the Normans of France that are credited with introducing the species to Britain during the 11th century. The development of colors was not to happen until about the 16th century, by which time the rabbit had become an established inhabitant of monasteries. It can thus be said that the monks of England, France, and other European countries were the first people to really advance the development of the breeds.

By the 17th century, the breeding of these easily maintained lagomorphs had become the common people's firmly established means of obtaining both meat and fur. However, the development of the rabbit fancy as such and the proliferation of the breeds are much more recent occurrences. They are a consequence of the dramatic social changes that took place in Britain and Europe during the 19th century. At this time there was much interest in the breeding of all kinds of species as pets and exhibition subjects. Clubs were formed, and breeders were quick to appreciate the value of any rabbit that was somewhat different from contemporary rabbit breeds. The rabbit was exported from Europe to most parts of the world during the 18th and 19th centuries, and during these years it arrived in the USA and Australia in vast numbers. In Australia and on many islands, its effect was devastating on the environment, due to a lack of natural rabbit-predators, and is possibly the worst example of human error in transplanting a species. To this day, the state of Queensland does not permit the general keeping of rabbits as pets, though they are now permitted in all other Australian states. As the 20th century got underway,

For centuries, rabbits have been kept as pets. All domestic rabbits are descendants of the Old World wild rabbit *Oryctolagus cuniculus.*

Rabbits can make wonderful pets for people of all ages, and their requirements are simple when compared to other pets such as dogs and cats. (The breed shown here, the Mini Lop, along with another "mini" breed, the Mini Rex, is included in this book on the basis that they are "dwarfs" in comparison to their larger counterparts whose name they share.)

the hobby expanded at a considerable pace and resulted in most of the varieties that are the foundation stock of today's breeds. All of the colors, patterns, coat changes, and anatomical deviations from the wild rabbit are the result of mutations. These mutations have been propagated as a direct consequence of the greater understanding of the science of genetics, which began to have an impact on all livestock breeding during the early years of this century.

THE VIRTUES OF RABBITS

The rabbit has proved itself to be a very durable pet. This is because it offers so many advantages to its owner. It is very quiet, and so it will not annoy the neighbors with a raucous voice—as might pets such as dogs and parrots. It will not run about terrifying old people and children as might a dog, and its initial cost and needs will not be as expensive as they could be if you purchased tropical fish or an aviary of birds. It has no body odor and is simplicity itself in its requirements for feeding and general care.

If rabbits are handled gently and often, they become extremely affectionate pets that will follow you around your home or your garden. (Naturally, a garden should be well fenced.) If fed and managed correctly, these little mammals may live up to ten years of age. They are, of course, loved by all children and can get on just fine with most other pets if they are introduced early on and properly supervised. Apart from their many benefits as house pets, they also make challenging exhibition animals that will not break your purse strings in owning a few quality examples.

If the idea of breeding appeals to you, then rabbits have few peers. The vast number of colors and patterns available means that there is tremendous scope to specialize in one or more of them. There is in all

western countries a network of national, regional, and local clubs that cater to the rabbit fancy. This means that there is a strong social side to the hobby, in which you can meet with others who share your love of these little furry friends. Whatever level at which you wish to participate, you will find that it is catered to in the rabbit fancy.

In this book, all the essential information that you are likely to need in order to obtain and care for a dwarf rabbit and to get underway as a pet owner, exhibitor, or breeder will be found. From this basic start, you can build up your knowledge by referring to more detailed works and by active participation in the fancy. Although the text is directed specifically for those interested in obtaining a dwarf rabbit, the care

chapters are equally applicable to any rabbit, providing that consideration is made to the larger breeds in respect to housing and nutritional needs. Naturally, the needs of larger breeds would be somewhat more voluminous than would those of the dwarf breeds.

WHAT IS A DWARF RABBIT?

There is no official definition of what constitutes a dwarf rabbit, and only three breeds bear the word *dwarf* in their names: the Netherland Dwarf, the Dwarf Hotot, and the Dwarf Lop. The dictionary defines a dwarf as any animal that is smaller than the

Left: Mini Lop, a pint-sized version of the large lop-type rabbit.
Below: Despite their small size, dwarf rabbits are hardy little animals.

average size of the population. Genetically, dwarfism is the result of recessive genes that alter the anatomical structure of an animal so that parts of its body become shorter. Dwarfism is a very variable feature in that, in some instances, it can be a lethal or semi-lethal feature. This means that the dwarfs die at birth or as juveniles. In other instances, the effect of this genetic state is not lethal, and the dwarfs live normal lives but may suffer to a greater or lesser degree from negative side effects that are a consequence of the anatomical changes. There are thus a number of different kinds of dwarfs.

Achondroplasia (the foreshortening of limbs) is seen in a number of dog breeds, such as the dachshund and the bulldog, and is not uncommon in cattle and other farm livestock. In rabbits, true dwarfism is a lethal genetic characteristic. What we see in the dwarf rabbits is not the genetic form known to exist in the species but an example of what is called quantitative inheritance of multiple genes. It is a build-up of genes for smallness. If a dwarf rabbit is mated to a larger rabbit breed, the offspring will display a range of sizes between the two

Close-up of a Netherland Dwarf. The round head and short erect ears are characteristic of the breed.

parents. However, at the minimal size within the species rabbits do display an anatomical change in respect to their head shape, which is foreshortened and more domed. Any defects that apparently accompany the diminutive size of dwarfs, such as questionable disposition, dental problems, and so on are not a direct result of smallness. Rather, they reflect that the early stock used in the development of dwarf breeds was itself suspect in these areas. The situation was not made any better by the fact that a high degree of inbreeding was used to intensify the genes for small size. This practice tended to fix in any other problems that were extant in the stock being used.

Dwarf rabbit breeds lead healthy lives and pose no more problems to the pet owner than any other rabbit breeds. This was not always the case.

Early in their development, as discussed, they had a bad reputation for producing very unhealthy offspring, as well as having a poor breeding record. They also had a reputation for being aggressive in spite of their small size. Fortunately, the efforts of reputable enthusiasts in culling out undesirable breeding stock has dramatically improved these tiny rabbits.

In this book, the author has used the popular view of a dwarf rabbit in determining which breeds should be included. This means that, apart from the breeds that

Above and Below: Dedicated breeders have steadily improved the quality of dwarf-type rabbits through careful selection of breeding stock and culling of undesirable specimens.

Mini Lop.

A pair of Netherland Dwarfs. This breed is very popular on the show scene.

and the Rex, that have miniature counterparts (the Mini Lop and the Mini Rex, respectively). A miniature

have the word *dwarf* in their names, the Polish, the Britannia Petite, the Jersey Wooly, the Holland (Dwarf) Lop, and the American Fuzzy Lop can all be regarded as dwarfs. The Himalayan and Dutch, which may weigh only the same, or less, than a Fuzzy, are not dwarfs. Rather, they are small rabbits, by virtue of the fact that they show no anatomical deviations from the basic structure of the typical rabbit. Coincidentally, the dwarfs are all breeds with an upper-limit weight of 4 lbs., whereas the small rabbit breeds all have acceptable upper weights above this figure. A miniature is a breed that is a diminutive replica of a larger existing breed. There are presently two breeds, the Lop

may weigh more than numerous small rabbit breeds. However, it was felt that the inclusion of these two miniatures was justified in a work on dwarf breeds on the grounds that they are dwarfs when compared to the average size of their larger brothers whose names they share.

Given the small size of the dwarfs, it is

readily apparent that they make extremely good house pets, which no doubt accounts for their great popularity in urban situations. In the USA, the dwarf breeds account for a considerable number of annual registrations. The dwarfs are also excellent exhibition animals, the Netherland Dwarf in particular being highly popular wherever rabbits are on show.

A further advantage of this group of bunnies is that they do not breed in the proverbial numbers that most rabbits do. This may not seem like an advantage at first, but it is because it means you are not likely to be overrun with offspring of which you cannot easily dispose. Generally, breeders of dwarf rabbits have no problems locating homes for their surplus stock.

Housing

There are many types of commercially made rabbit cages on the market. Your pet shop dealer can help you select one that is just right for your pet.

The potential range of accommodations that can be provided for your rabbit is limited only by your imagination, space, and available funds. There are many factors to consider in deciding what is the best choice for your particular situation. For example, will you be keeping just one or two pets in your home, or will they be housed in an outdoor shed or other enclosed area? If you plan to breed, the housing will no doubt be very different to that in which just one or two pets are to be accommodated. In the latter situation, you can devote considerably more space to each pet than could a breeder.

However, when you bring housing needs down to the individual rabbit, there are certain basic considerations that are applicable to all rabbits, regardless of whether you are keeping only a few or

an entire breeding colony. They are that the hutch or cage should be spacious, well constructed, easily cleaned, located in an area that is draft free, and, most importantly, well ventilated with fresh air. Clearly, if a rabbit home is to be within your own home or in a building, it need not be of such rugged construction as a hutch that is placed in an outdoor location.

ALL-WIRE CAGES AND SIZE

The most popular method of housing rabbits today is in all-wire cages. They offer the benefits of ease in cleaning, relatively low-cost purchase, and provide few places in which parasites can multiply. They can be added to with ease to form stacks—an obvious advantage to the breeder. They come in a range of sizes and furnishings. Some are simply a rectangular galvanized unit with no equipment; others include a sliding refuse tray and urine deflector. Legs may be included with the cage, or they may be an extra charge.

The cage size for a dwarf rabbit would not, in theory, need to be as large as one for the bigger breeds. This said, you should take into account other factors. For example, if the rabbit is to spend most of its time in the cage, the cage should be as large as cash permits. If your pet is to be allowed the freedom of a shed or your home, the cage is merely a place in which to sleep and eat, so it need not be of great size. As a guide to minimum size, think in terms of 24x15x15 in. (61x38x38cm), and increase this if two bunnies are to share the cage.

The fact that cages and hutches are manufactured within a certain size range does not mean that they are ideal housing for rabbits but reflects the balance between basic suitability and the unit costs of producing them, which obviously must appeal to the average rabbit keeper.

This cage is too small to serve as permanent housing, but it is sufficient for purposes of transportation, e.g., veterinary visits.

A dwarf rabbit is a spry little animal. It is, therefore, important that it is handled securely when being taken out of or placed into its cage.

manufacturers who advertise in the rabbit magazines.

OUTDOOR AND INDOOR HUTCHES

The hutch is the traditional home for a rabbit. It is more aesthetic-ally pleasing compared to the clinical look of an all-wire cage and offers the rabbit a greater sense of security. In an outdoor situation, it is the only form of accommodations that should be considered. It must be constructed of stout timber or an equally suitable material of a minimum ½-in. thickness. The roof should slope and be well covered with a waterproof felt. It should overhang the walls of the hutch so that they are given

Above: If you want to keep more than one rabbit, you must plan accordingly for accommodations that will be roomy enough for the occupants.

If you are keeping only one or two pets but wish to restrict their movement in your home, then you can easily assemble a run by stapling galvanized wire to a wooden frame. All-wire cages are not at all suited to outdoor use, even if they are protected within a wooden shelter framework. Most pet shops stock models of all-wire cages; but if not, there are a number of speciality

The exterior of the outdoor hutch should be treated periodically with a wood protective: doing so will help to minimize damage from the elements.

protection against adverse weather.

The hutch should be raised about 12 in. (31cm) minimum above the ground to allow plenty of fresh air to circulate under the floor. The hutch can either be divided so that a darkened sleeping area—with an external door—is provided, or a sleeping box of suitable size can be placed in the hutch, assuming that the hutch is of good dimension. The front can be made of galvanized wire mounted on a hinged or removable frame. A slideable refuse tray can be fitted under the bottom of the cage. (Some hobbyists opt for a solid floor that has been well coated with a suitable gloss paint—for ease of cleaning–but this option requires nothing less than *meticulous* maintenance to prevent health and sanitation problems.) Wall protection against urine splash can be facilitated with the use of a 6-in. (15cm) guard made of transparent, weather-resistant thermoplastic. Pieces of this material can be screwed to the back and side walls, making their removable easy when the interior is repainted.

For added protection against inclement weather, a

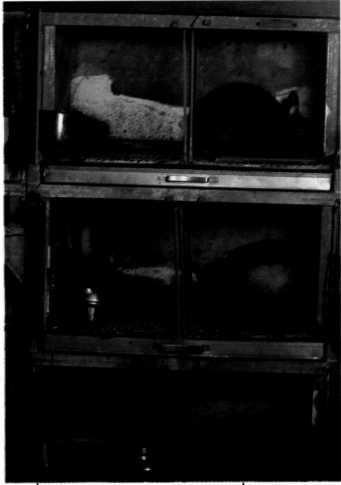

sheet of thermoplastic can be fitted over the wire front. A series of holes along the top of it, combined with similar holes in the back wall of the hutch (just below roof level), will ensure a supply of fresh air.

The floor can have a generous covering of white untreated wood shavings over either a few layers of paper or over sawdust. The sleeping quarters should be amply supplied with quality hay during the colder months, less

Section of a rabbitry housing Netherland Dwarf rabbits.

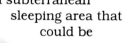

Above: A nicely designed outdoor hutch. It provides for an ample play and exercise area and an enclosed sleeping area. Note that the roof is sloped to prevent the accumulation of rain water. **Below:** A quartet of Mini Rexes.

so in spring through summer. This bedding will, of course, be eaten on a daily basis, so it must be replenished. The exterior of the outdoor hutch must either be painted or covered with a good wood protective, which will ensure a long hutch life if it is periodically recoated.

The indoor hutch is modeled in the same manner, but less substantial timber can be used; and a roof overhang is, of course, unnecessary. The hutch may have a wire floor so that droppings can fall through onto a tray, though I have never liked placing

any animal on a wire floor. I feel that doing so is totally unnatural and offers only the advantage of ease in cleaning. Further, the rabbit is denied the natural habit of eating its cecal pellets.

The hutch offers the imaginative pet owner ample room for scope in making it an interesting home. It is possible to make a resting platform above floor level if height permits. You can also provide a subterranean sleeping area that could be accessed

from the main floor of the hutch. The exterior of the hutch can be made to look like a cottage or a castle by simply adding a wooden facade. Children love this, and it makes the hutch less utilitarian in appearance.

BREEDING ROOMS

The potential breeder is well advised to give the breeding room very careful thought. It via ducts at floor and ceiling levels. Beware of any cages that might become overly hot due to direct sunlight falling on them. This would really stress the rabbits.

Light, heat, a cooling unit, and water service will prove a boon in the breeding room. Floors should be of the easy-clean type. If a shed is used, you can save on heating bills by insulating the walls. To

An outdoor exercise run. The occupant (a non-dwarf rabbit) has the opportunity to nibble on the grass in the spring and summer months.

should be designed to accommodate tiers of hutches that are on castors. If this is done, the hutches can easily be moved away from the walls to facilitate cleaning. Always allow for ample work surfaces and storage cupboards. Ventilation should be provided keep dust and airborne bacteria to a minimum, it is advisable to install a suitably sized ionizer. There are many models from which you can choose, they are economical to run, and their efficacy has been proven in use by bird and small-mammal breeders.

Sadly, in this day and age, you must make sure that the breeding room is well secured with strong padlocks or even an alarm system if cash permits. An external night light should be regarded as essential for the breeding room if it is a detached building outside of your home.

EXERCISE AREAS

Regardless of whether you keep just one pet rabbit or are a breeder with a number of rabbits, provision must be made to provide the stock with an exercise area. Breeders tend to neglect this aspect of husbandry on the grounds that they have too many rabbits to care for; thus, they have neither the time nor the facility to let their stock run loose. This is unfortunate and suggests that the needs of the stock are secondary to the need to keep large numbers of rabbits.

If you get great pleasure from your rabbits, then every effort should be made to ensure that they enjoy life as well. The single-rabbit owner can easily construct a good-sized run in a garden, where his pet can scamper around (under supervision, of course). Alternatively, a wire coop can be made that has a mesh over it so that the rabbit(s) can be left unattended and are protected from the attentions of dogs, cats, foxes, and their like. It can be moved around on a lawn so that the pets can browse on the fresh grass.

A breeder can construct a more permanent outdoor exercise area that is divided into runs. The benefits of such a facility to the stock are considerable. The animals will be more hardy, and they will certainly maintain better

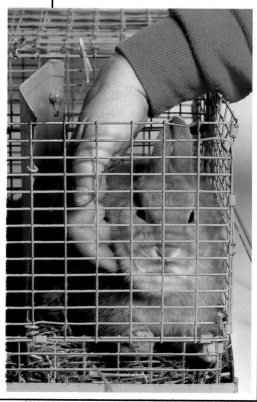

condition. They will really enjoy their outings in the exercise area. The pet owner who wants the ultimate accommodations for the outdoor-kept rabbit might utilize a bird-aviary style home, where the run is full-height mesh; and the shed or shelter is the indoor home in which the pet has the entire floor area to sleep upon. Both the shelter and the run can be furnished with attractions such as rocks, logs, tunnels, and their like.

Keeping a pet rabbit should not be a case of simply restricting the pet to a cage but providing the sort of accommodations that the bunny will really love and that will be a constant source of pride and interest to you as the designer. The more freedom your pets have the more you will see aspects of their characters that simply are not evident in those animals that are kept in cages or hutches for most of their lives.

A Netherland Dwarf of lynx coloration.

Selecting Dwarf Rabbits

The way in which you should go about selecting one or more dwarf rabbits will be influenced by a number of factors that should be given much thought beforehand. If they are not, there is a very strong possibility that you will be unhappy with what you purchase. If you have never owned a rabbit before, it is even more imperative that you give special considerations to these factors, a discussion of which follows.

not important, but simply a matter of personal preference, that its quality be anything special, as long as it is an obvious example of the breed that you like and is very healthy. Such a bunny can be purchased at a young age, a factor that, no doubt, will be important to you. If you wish to become a breeder, then you will need to be much more careful that you obtain quality stock.

Rabbits of good breeding potential may not necessarily

Mini Rexes. Before you acquire your rabbit, you should decide whether you want simply an animal of pet quality or one that you can breed and/or show. There are quite a few dwarf rabbit breeds from which you can choose and each has its own unique appeal.

THE OBJECTIVE OF OWNERSHIP

You must decide before all else what the main reason is why you want to own a dwarf rabbit. If the animal is to be purely a household pet it is

be good show prospects, no more than a winning show-rabbit is necessarily a good breeding animal. So, first of all, decide on the purpose of your purchase.

CHOICE OF BREED AND COLOR

These considerations are related to personal preferences and availability. However, certain practical facts should also be kept in mind. For example, if you do not enjoy grooming, then it would seem pointless to obtain a Jersey Wooly or an American Fuzzy Lop. Likewise, it must be appreciated that the pendulate ears of the lops need more careful attention in terms of their general care. They are more prone to cuts and abrasions as well as to ear problems resulting from ear parasites or from secondary infections as a result of cuts.

The availability of a given breed is related to the country in which you live. Those in the USA have the best choice, followed by those in Canada, and then Britain. Australians are at a disadvantage with most pets due to the size of their country. Of course, with rabbits they are at a special disadvantage as these pets are still in the early stages of being accepted. This is due to the past destructive history of rabbits on Australian grazing lands.

If you are British and wish to exhibit your dwarfs,

then obviously you cannot own, for example, a Jersey Wooly or Dwarf Hotot, as these breeds are not as yet recognized in Britain. Likewise, if you live in one of the more remote states of the USA, such as New Mexico or Utah, there may not be quite the same opportunity to be an active exhibitor of Dwarf Hotots or Britannia Petites as if you lived in a more populous state or region. This being so, one of the highly

A Netherland Dwarf in a typically alert stance. Netherland Dwarfs are one of the best known breeds of dwarf rabbit.

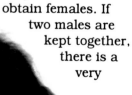

Jersey Wooly.

popular dwarfs might be a better choice.

Conversely, if you are more interested in the breeding side of dwarfs, there could be a singular advantage in taking on one of the less popular breeds. You would no doubt be the only source of supply for your chosen breed for many miles around, indeed one of the few breeders in the entire region. Some colors and patterns are much more popular than are others, so availability will be a factor here as well. Another factor that can favor a less popular breed is that when you do compete, you may have, statistically, a better

chance of winning than in the highly competitive breeds. You may thus be able to establish yourself as a leading breeder much faster than if you are taking on the top breeders of the popular breeds. If you simply adore all dwarfs, there still remain very real practical aspects to consider before deciding on a breed or color.

WHICH IS THE BEST SEX?

If the dwarf is to be a pet, then it really does not matter which sex you obtain as both are equally affectionate. If you wish to own two or more pet rabbits, then you should obtain females. If two males are kept together, there is a very

strong chance that they will fight, and this likelihood will be assured if they should scent a doe in the area. Females will, of course, have their little quarrels, but they do not fight with the same level of tenacity as do males competing for courtship rights. If two males are reared together, they can become great pals; but it is wiser overall to have does if your pets are to live together.

If you plan to be a breeder, then obviously you will need females. Initially, there is no need to own a buck at all. You can always utilize the services of the males of top breeders to cover your does. However, if you live a long way from an established breeder, then there would be merit in purchasing a good stud buck with your initial two or three does.

WHAT AGE TO PURCHASE?

A pet bunny can be purchased anytime after it is about eight weeks old. By this age, it should be feeding well on its own. If it is younger than this, you could encounter many more problems. The fact that a shop or breeder is prepared to sell rabbits at an age younger than about eight weeks in no way means this is a desirable age to acquire one. If you wish to be a breeder, your options are to purchase youngsters, or to obtain young adults, or to acquire more mature stock that is not over the hill in breeding terms. The best choice is the second option, obtaining either proven breeders (the more costly approach) or proven stock in respect to

A rabbit should be eight weeks old at the very least before it goes to its new home.

Dwarf rabbits don't require spacious accommodations. Thus, even those who live in apartments can enjoy the pleasures of these delightful little animals.

If you are planning to get involved in showing your rabbit, it is a good idea to visit a few rabbit shows before you make your final selection. This will enable you to get an idea of what a good example of your chosen breed should look like.

its adjudged quality. Obtaining very young rabbits is the least costly way to proceed, but, of course, you are taking a gamble as to whether or not they will mature into well-colored or well-marked adults.

Mature breeding stock, when available, can be a very worthwhile investment if a reputable breeder is thinning down the older rabbits in order to make way for younger prospects.

THE COST FACTOR

The cost of a dwarf rabbit will reflect its age, quality, breed, and place of purchase. In fact, there are many factors that will influence the price, so it is not possible to be specific. The price will depend on whether you

are purchasing a pet-quality rabbit or a quality rabbit that may have already done some winning or is already a proven reproducer of winning or quality stock. The very best rabbits in a given breed can exchange hands for substantial sums of money. The controlling factor is whether or not a breeder wants to part with a particular individual and how much you are prepared to offer in an attempt to persuade him to do so! Generally, you should not attempt to enter into this type of situation because you will probably end up paying more than you should and will not have the experience to make the best of such outstanding specimens, even if you owned them. A potential breeder should ask around to establish what a fair price is. He should then obtain

Dwarf Hotot. As with many other animals, prices for dwarf rabbits will vary. Breed, age, and quality all factor in to what you will pay for your pet.

stock of this caliber and try to build from it. Never try to buy breeding stock by saying that you only want a good-quality

pet. You will get exactly that: a very nice pet but certainly not one up to good breeding standard. Yet time and again beginners try to cut cost corners only to regret it down the line when they produce only mediocre offspring.

WHERE TO PURCHASE

Naturally, most people think of their local pet shop as a source of dwarf rabbits. Keep in

mind, however, that a pet shop dealer may not always be able to stock every dwarf rabbit variety that is available. In that case, you might consider contacting a dwarf rabbit breeder. If you are interested in the exhibition side of the hobby, make it a point to visit rabbit shows. Doing so will give you an idea of what constitutes a good specimen of the breed that you want to own. (Remember that a rabbit that is to be shown must be registered with your national rabbit registry and must come with a pedigree.)

It is always best to see potential breeding stock firsthand so that you can see the overall quality of all the stock owned by a breeder.

WHEN IS THE BEST TIME TO PURCHASE?

Rabbits are bred throughout the year thanks to artificial light and heat facilities. However, spring and summer are the ideal times to acquire young stock. In the warmer

If possible, try to purchase your dwarf rabbit sometime during the spring or summer months: fresh greenery will be readily available for bunny to munch on and he will also enjoy his time spent outdoors.

This cute trio exhibits but a few of the many colors in which dwarf rabbits are available.

The dwarf rabbit that you purchase should be fully furred and should not exhibit any bald patches.

likely health will be the conditions in which the rabbits live. If they are cramped, smelly, and dirty you need not waste your time further—find another supplier. Amazingly, this obvious advice is often ignored by beginners—at their own expense when their pets quickly go down with a fatal illness. Disreputable breeders and dealers can survive only because, in plain language, there is always a flow of unsuspecting customers who will purchase their poorly-cared-for stock.

months, there will be ample homegrown vegetables and other green foods available, and you will be able to enjoy seeing your rabbit play in your garden. Purchase during the colder months only if you have adequate heated indoor accommodations available or if your rabbit is to live in your home as a pet.

ASSESSING HEALTH

Regardless of its quality, the singular most important attribute of a newly purchased dwarf is that it is in the peak of health. If you purchase from a reputable source, this will be the case. However, you should still know how to spot an unwell rabbit. Your first guide to

A healthy specimen should meet certain criteria, regardless of its age or breed. If it does not, then it has a problem—be it of a temporary nature or something much more serious. Never accept a rabbit that is in anything other than perfect health—regardless of whether you are told that a condition is only minor and will disappear within a day or two.

Netherland Dwarf. A healthy rabbit is bright-eyed, alert, and interested in its surroundings.

The rabbit should be observed as it moves around. Its movement should be done in any easy hopping manner, with no signs whatsoever of impediment to limb movement. If you are satisfied on this account, it can be held and given a physical check. The ears should be clean and display no signs of brown wax inside of them; there should not be any smell other than one of freshness. The eyes should be bright and clear with no signs of staining around them, let alone liquid being discharged from them. The nose should be dry and should not discharge liquid. It should not in any way be swollen on either nostril. Be especially watchful for any signs of dampness on the sides of the face and the paws: these conditions could indicate the serious illness known as snuffles.

Inspect the teeth very carefully or have the seller do this for you. The teeth should be white, clean, and, most important, aligned correctly. A rabbit's teeth grow throughout its life. The upper incisors are kept to the correct length by the foods that the rabbit gnaws on, while those of the lower jaw rub against those of the upper jaw. If this alignment is not correct, the lower teeth can

A rabbit's ears should be clean and free of any unpleasant odor. This holds true for all rabbits but especially so for those with lop ears.

A rabbit's teeth should align correctly and should not exhibit any discoloration. Some breeds are more prone to tooth problems than are others.

If rabbits are tense or alarmed, they often will nestle together to feel secure.

Mini Lop.

behind them. Any rabbit breed can suffer from continue growing up and into the upper jaw. In this case the condition is known as overshot. The condition known as undershot occurs when the lower incisors protrude past the upper incisors. In this case, the uppers will grow down through the lower jaw. In either of these situations, the rabbit will have great difficulty in eating and could starve. The lower incisors should just touch those of the upper jaw but be slightly malocclusion of the teeth, but it is a problem of particular note with dwarfs due to the foreshortening of the skull, which can create changes in the arrangement of the jaws. Some breeds and strains are more prone to the problem than others, so it behooves you to check this point very carefully. In the event that an apparently normal-toothed dwarf should later develop problems, you can have your vet trim the teeth periodically. Do not ignore this need. You should never breed a dwarf once malocclusion has been established.

When checking the fur, brush it against its lie with your hand to see if any parasites are seen scurrying for

Jersey Wooly. Keep in mind that a wool-coated rabbit will require more grooming care than will a short-haired specimen.

cover. Fleas move quickly; lice move very slowly. The dark specks that might be seen are the fecal matter of these parasites. Be on the lookout for any bald spots on the body, and be sure to inspect the rabbit's underbelly for sores, swellings, and abrasions. The fur should impart total health and be dense in all breeds. Check the hocks to see that they are fully furred.

Inspect the anal region to ensure that it is not stained, which would suggest an existing or recent problem. Needless to say, the sight of congealed fecal matter around the rear end is not a sign of good health or management. If you plan to exhibit your stock, be sure that all the toes are present and that the ears have no pieces missing from them! The rabbit has five digits on each foot, but one of them, the dewclaw, is small and does not touch the floor.

If all of the advice given in this chapter is followed, you should be assured of a dwarf rabbit that meets all of your expectations. Remember to ask the seller exactly what foods the rabbit has been eating and try to supply them over at least the first two weeks before making any changes. When any animal goes to a new home, it is a traumatic experience. By maintaining the same feeding regimen until the animal is well settled, there will be one less problem to overcome.

Feeding Rabbits

Rabbits are extremely easy pets to cater to in terms of their nutritional needs. They are herbivores, which means their diet should consist of foods of plant origin— vegetables, fruits, wild plants, grain crops, and seeds. Apart from the fresh foods mentioned, you can also feed wet or dry mashes. They are simply concoctions that an owner puts

Netherland Dwarfs. Feeding a rabbit is a fairly straight-forward matter. A combination of greenfoods and dryfood form the basic core of the diet.

youngsters a few days old through to post-weaning, those that are for maintenance diets, and those that are for good wool growth or for the show rabbit. But you need not get too carried away by the label claims of a particular formula because any of the leading producers' pelleted rabbit foods will be

just fine for your stock.

together and in which the various essential compounds are included. The essential constituents of food are proteins, fats, carbohydrates, vitamins, and minerals. Water, of course, is the final and most important item in any feeding regimen.

Apart from fresh foods, many proprietary diets have been developed over the years by companies that specialize in rabbit nutrition. There are commercial foods for

The advantages of feeding commercial pellets over fresh foods is that the pellets are carefully formulated to contain each of the essential ingredients (in a consistent ratio) needed by a rabbit. Pellets thus take a lot of the guesswork out of feeding, and they are also very convenient and easy to store. However, your rabbits will really enjoy fresh foods. In numerous tests that this author conducted

with his stock, the rabbits always preferred fresh foods to pelleted foods.

The prudent rabbit keeper should therefore endeavor to take advantage of both pelleted foods and those that are fresh and very appealing to a rabbit. Look at it this way: a pelleted food does not allow your stock to be selective over what ingredients it eats. This is a big plus in that a rabbit cannot gobble up lots of given foods because it likes their taste yet which are not providing it with all of the ingredients needed for good metabolism. Conversely, a pelleted food is very concentrated and does not meet the

rabbit's psychological need to browse and eat steadily as it would in the wild. By feeding a regimen of pellets supplemented with fresh food, your rabbit will receive an excellent diet that meets its metabolic needs, as well as being enjoyable and something to which it looks forward.

FRESH GREENFOODS

The list of fresh greenfoods that your pet will enjoy is almost unlimited. Apples are always a favored item, pears rarely so. Lettuce is well liked, but it has a high water-content and so has little nutritional content. Celery, green beans, and peas are

American Fuzzy Lop. The greenfoods that you feed your rabbit should be of the freshest quality.

Netherland Dwarf. Your rabbit's food bowl should be non-tippable. Food bowls made of crockery, which are available at your pet shop, are your best choice.

This mixture contains a variety of dry food items including rabbit-food pellets, corn, and oats.

An appetizing assortment of some foods that rabbits enjoy. Also pictured is a gravity-fed water bottle, which is the ideal way to provide water for your rabbit—it prevents the animal from soiling its water.

usually enjoyed; and, of course, all rabbits enjoy carrots. Cress and spinach are very useful plants to include in a diet. Many fruits can be tried and will be taken with a varying degree of relish. Among wild plants, dandelions are favored, as are chickweed, parsley, shepherd's purse, plantain, a variety of grasses, and many others. The flowering heads of many plants are also enjoyed, a point to remember if your rabbit is allowed a romp in your flower bed! Branches from fruit trees will be well received by rabbits. They provide excellent fiber as well as something to help keep the incisors in good shape and length. Never feed plants grown from bulbs, and avoid buttercups, lily of the valley, hemlock, deadly nightshade, and other poisonous plants. The golden rule is always that if you are in doubt, leave it out.

All greenfoods must be fresh. Never feed those that have yellow leaves or are clearly overripe. Wash all greenfoods to remove any residual chemicals that may have been sprayed onto them as these substances may be toxic to your pet. You must never feed any greenfoods in a glut simply because they are suddenly available in quantity. Doing so will almost certainly result in scours, or diarrhea. Introduce greenfoods slowly into the diet, and do likewise with any foods that the rabbit has never previously tasted.

You can supply your pet with one or two types of greenfood each day so that a balanced variety is given over any one week, or you can supply a mixed salad of vegetables and fruits. You will soon get to know which greenfoods are favored items because they are always the first to be eaten. Rabbits that are fed a mixed diet will really look forward to each day's menu to see what it contains. They will run to and fro, shaking their heads in excitement when you approach their cage, hutch, or compound.

DRY FOODS

Under this heading come all grain foods and their by-products, such as bread, biscuits, and other similar items. Crushed oats are the standard form of grain food, along with bran. But all cereal crops are eaten and can be given along with oats and bran. Rabbits will enjoy many seeds, such as millet and sunflower, as well as shelled nuts. Dry bread is good for your pet as it provides something for him to gnaw on. Even though rabbits do enjoy cookies and cake, they should not be fed such sweet items. Never feed chocolate and candies to them as these sweets have no benefits at all and will adversely affect rabbits' teeth just as they will your own.

You can purchase bags of mixed rabbit food from your

Your dwarf rabbit will enjoy being fed bits of dry bread. This will give him the opportunity to exercise his teeth, which grow continuously throughout his lifetime.

pet shop. If you keep a large number of rabbits, it might be more economical to buy the cereals separately and make up your own mix. However, when purchasing any grain in quantity, be very sure that it is stored correctly. Keep it in a darkened dry cupboard and in a container that is not

meat extracts, shredded cheese, crumbled wholemeal bread, porridge oats, boiled potatoes, grated carrots, and so on.

In past years, damp mash was a key part of the diet for breeding does as it ensured that they received the important proteins essential to nursing females. Damp

Store dry food in a dark dry cupboard; store greenfoods appropriately so that they don't spoil.

exposed to either the air or rodents. You should pick your grain supplier with care. Support those who clearly have steady business, which ensures that they have a steady turnover of stock. If any grain seems moldy or in any way contaminated with rodent droppings, you would be wise to locate a new supplier.

MASH FOODS

A mash can be made of dry foods, or it can be dampened with a liquid such as warm water, meat stock, or milk. In its damp state, it should be just moist enough to bind the ingredients together, never to be a sloppy mash that your pet will not want. You can add all kinds of ingredients to a damp mash. They would include hard-boiled egg yolk,

mashes are not as popular today because they are time consuming in preparation and have a short feed-life. If they are not eaten within a few hours, they must be removed; otherwise, they will sour and be harmful to the rabbit.

However, if you have only a few rabbits, they make for an interesting addition to the diet. Vitamin supplements can be sprinkled onto them, as can powdered calcium for the pregnant and nursing doe. Alternatively, the female can be given wholemeal bread soaked in milk during the breeding period. A word of caution, however, with respect to vitamin supplements. They are not needed if your rabbit receives a balanced diet. They can cause hypervitaminosis, which is an excess of certain vitamins. This condition can create health hazards, so supplements are best given only after veterinary consultation in order to meet a particular need. Giving them for no reason is poor husbandry.

If the basic diet consists of pellets, remember that the water intake of the rabbit will increase, so this precious liquid must always be present on an ad lib basis, and it must be fresh. A final food item that is essential for rabbits and that makes fine bedding as well is good-quality meadow hay. It can be purchased in bags from your pet store or in bales from a farmer or grain merchant. It must smell fresh and never be moldy as mold can cause serious diseases in rabbits.

From the foregoing you will see that it is not difficult to provide your pet with an interesting diet that is a mixture of fresh food items and pellets. The exact amount of one to the other is a matter of personal preference and observation of the health of your pet. If a given pet seems to be getting overweight, you can cut down on the carbohydrates, such as oats and bran, while maintaining the pellet ration. It may take some weeks to bring weight under control so never try to starve the rabbit into weight loss. This is a very foolish way to proceed and will certainly result in the bunny being placed at health risk. Your pet should never be either over or under weight as both conditions will affect its general well being and, ultimately, its life expectancy.

Netherland Dwarf. The amount of food that a dwarf rabbit will eat will vary from breed to breed. Naturally, dwarfs will consume less food than their bigger brothers.

Dry food can be made available to your pet at all times. Greenfoods spoil much more quickly and therefore should not be left in the feeding area for prolonged periods of time.

A hay rack is a very useful addition to your rabbit's cage. It allows for hay to be easily available for your pet to nibble on but prevents him from soiling the hay with his droppings.

WHEN TO FEED

Dry foods can be left freely available at all times, as can hay. Mashes are best given either in the morning or in the late afternoon as this avoids the hottest part of the day, when they will sour more quickly. For this same reason, fresh foods are also best given in the morning or later in the day.

FEEDING UTENSILS

For a single pet rabbit, the best food containers (for dry and fresh foods) are rabbit pots made of crockery, which are available at your pet shop. Water can also be given in a crockery pot, or it can be supplied via a gravity-fed water bottle that is suspended at a convenient height from the inside front of the cage. Such bottles, which prevent a rabbit from soiling its water, come in a range of sizes and models. You can purchase garden hose nozzles that allow the hose to be used for replenishing water if many rabbits are kept.

If you plan to keep a number of breeding rabbits, naturally you will need a number of cages or hutches. In that case, you might find it worthwhile investing in an automatic watering system. There are many models from which to choose. They operate by having a central cylinder of water that feeds a pipeline, which has a terminal in each cage. Each pipeline terminal is equipped with a water spout that is easily activated by the rabbit's licking it. Such systems can also be fed from

the main water supply. A hay rack is a useful item, as is an automatic dry-food dispenser. The food dispenser can be

attached to the exterior of the cage, thus saving time in replenishing food bowls and saving space in the cage. It may result in less food being scattered out of a container by the scratching action of rabbits when they feed.

The feeding of your rabbit should be an interesting part of keeping your little pet, never a chore. If you keep a number of rabbits, it is essential that you have sufficient time to observe each of them as they feed. Your knowledge of your pet's feeding behavior can be important in giving you advance warning of an impending illness.

COPROPHAGY

Rabbits, hares, and rodents such as guinea pigs practice a form of food intake that is known as coprophagy. In this process, partly digested pellets are voided from the body via the anus and eaten. These partially digested bits are called cecal pellets. They should not be confused with fecal matter, which might be the case if you were unaware of this special form of redigestion. The process enables the rabbit to maximize on the vegetation that it eats: it helps to break down the strong cellulose walls of the vegetation. Humans overcome the same problem by boiling vegetables. Cows do it by regurgitation of foods (chewing the cud), and birds ingest small grit particles to break down cellulose into a paste.

Rabbit snacks such as hay cubes are available at most pet shops.

An attractive pair of Polish examining an array of treats.

General Care

Rabbits are very straightforward pets to care for in terms of their general husbandry. The application of basic knowledge plus a good helping of common sense should ensure that they live trouble-free lives. The initial advice to a newcomer is that his rabbit's accommodations should be prepared in advance of the animal's arrival. A small quantity of dry foods and pellets should have been purchased, as well as all necessary food and water containers. This means that nothing needs to be purchased in a panic; you have time to obtain the housing and utensils that you want, rather than settling for what is available at the last minute.

BRINGING YOUR RABBIT HOME

Try to bring your new pet home as early in the day as possible so that it has time to settle into its quarters before

nightfall. If you have purchased a cage (to be used for your pet's home), it can be used to transport the bunny; otherwise, a stiff cardboard box amply lined with hay will be fine. Scatter a few pellets or oats and some sliced apple in whatever is used as the travel cage if the journey is of more than one hour's duration. Doing so will enable the animal to eat and to obtain liquid. Never leave a rabbit in a hot vehicle as it will get badly stressed. Go straight home once you have obtained your pet. Once you are at home, place the rabbit in its quarters, give it food and water, and leave it awhile so that it can settle in.

HANDLING

It is very important that young children are taught from the outset how to

A cage such as this is ideal for transporting bunny to his new home. Notice that the bottom has been lined with hay.

handle and respect a little rabbit. Never pick a rabbit up by its ears. The only reason the ears need to be held at all is to steady and control the animal as you slide your hand under its body to lift it. It should then be brought to your chest so it is secure, leaving your other hand free to stroke it.

Children must be taught to never grab at a dwarf rabbit or in any way pull it about. Rabbits are basically timid little creatures, and they are very gentle by nature. But if any animal is hurt by mishandling, it will sooner or later bite in order to defend itself. It is unfortunate that a number of adults simply do not accept the proper responsibility for the pets that they bring into their homes and allow them to be mauled by children not old enough to appreciate the importance of gentle handling. Do not become one of these people.

RABBITS AND OTHER PETS

If you own a dog, a cat, or a ferret, you should understand that rabbits are one of the food items of these animals. This means that such pets will instinctively chase and bite small bunnies. Dwarf rabbit breeds are especially at risk to other pets

Wool, or angora-type, breeds such as the Jersey Wooly require regular grooming to prevent the build-up of excess hair.

American Fuzzy Lop.

Grooming time for this Jersey Wooly. Grooming programs should begin early on so that your pet will have plenty of time to get accustomed to—or at least tolerate—being groomed.

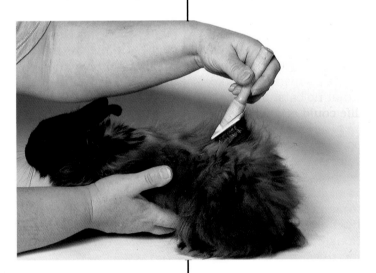

because of their diminutive size and nervous disposition. Never leave other pets alone with your rabbit until you are absolutely sure as to how they get on with each other. In a moment of high excitement, a dog or ferret could easily kill your little pet. You must carefully monitor the reaction of other pets to your rabbit. First, put the rabbit in its cage and let the other pet see it from a safe distance. Then, take things from there.

Only you know the character of your other pets. If kittens and puppies are brought up with rabbits, they will become close friends. I would never, however, trust a ferret with a rabbit, even though such friendships have been established.

POTENTIAL DANGERS

Regardless of how your rabbit is accommodated, the moment it is allowed freedom to exercise out of its cage it is at risk to many dangers that should be considered in advance.

Dangers in the Home

Baby rabbits may nibble at many things to see if they are edible so always be sure that electrical wires are not trailing and plugged into sockets. Beware of any fireplaces that are not suitably guarded with a safety screen. Be especially careful when you are working in the kitchen and bunny is hopping around: you can easily trip over him. Rabbits are not likely to pull on the cord of an iron situated on its board, but it would be wise not to have such a situation when your pet is running loose. Block off any potential hiding places, such as the area behind the refrigerator. Be sure that open balconies are safeguarded with sturdy mesh of some kind. A rabbit will not hurl itself off of such places; but if it were to be

startled, it could panic. This is the time when accidents and fatalities can occur.

Dangers in the Garden

Even baby rabbits are extremely fast-moving if frightened, so ensure that there is no risk that your pet might escape into a neighbor's yard or into open ground. Equally as important, make sure that no cats, dogs, or wildlife could attack them. Be aware of any poisonous plants that may be growing wild in your garden and remove them. Be sure that there are no piles of rocks, rubbish, or other materials under which your pet might creep and make it difficult for you to gather him up when fun time is over. Rotting piles of vegetation are a very real health hazard to rabbits: they develop colonies of bacteria and fungi that are airborne in transmission. Burn such vegetation or keep it in suitable containers if it is to be used as a fertilizer.

DANGERS IN THE BREEDING ROOM

Apart from diseases, the main risk to rabbits in the breeding room is if rodents gain entry and contaminate food. Snakes may also be a real risk, depending on the country in which you live. Check that all vents have a mesh cover of a maximum hole size of ¼ in. (73mm) square over them. Windows should be covered with small-size galvanized wire so that when they are open they are not accessible to unwanted animals.

American Fuzzy Lops.

A family of Mini Rexes.

ROUTINE HYGIENE

The reason for the vast majority of conditions and diseases in rabbits and other pets is lack of adequate hygiene. Good hygiene should incorporate every facet of husbandry—from stock levels in a given breeding room or cage, to feeding procedures, grooming, general cleaning, and personal hygiene

Jersey Wooly. Angora-type breeds should be groomed on a regular basis to keep them looking their best.

during handling or when in close proximity to rabbits. Pathogens (disease-causing organisms) can multiply in your rabbit's home, breeding room, or environment only if you let them. The following are key rules of routine hygiene:

1. Always store foods in a cool, dark, dry cupboard or room.

2. Always feed fresh foods. If you are unsure about the state of an opened bag of pellets, oats, or other packaged food, throw it out. The same applies to hay.

3. Wash and replenish water bowls daily. Do the same if you use gravity-fed water bottles, and be sure that the tips are also washed. Be sure that all utensils are thoroughly rinsed free of detergent.

4. Replace cracked or chipped feeding dishes as they can never be cleaned satisfactorily and could harbor pathogens.

5. Never leave fresh foods (greens, fruits, damp mashes) in the cage for more than twelve hours; otherwise, they will attract bacteria and other parasites. Uneaten foods like this cannot be offered again, so throw them away.

6. Ensure that cages and hutches are routinely cleaned at least once a week. Hutches should be periodically stripped down and repainted. Old paint must be thoroughly removed, especially in the corners— where pathogens can congregate.

7. Inspect your stock once a week to see that it has no parasites, wounds, or other abrasions. The sooner a problem is spotted the easier it is to treat, and the chances are lesser that it will spread to other rabbits, or even other pets, that you might own. Groom your pets each week and be especially diligent with the angora-like breeds.

8. Always protect stock kept outdoors from extremes of weather. Rabbits cannot tolerate dampness and quickly become ill if subjected to it. Additionally, they cannot withstand high temperatures or direct sunlight except for relatively short periods of time. Thus, they must always be able to retreat to a shady area.

9. Breeders and exhibitors should be especially mindful of the fact that their stock is at considerably more risk to disease than are rabbits that are kept singly, doubly, or triplicately. This being so, they should provide for mandatory quarantine for every single rabbit that is added to their stud. No exceptions should be made, regardless of how good their source.

10. Breeders with large studs should exercise due diplomatic care as to whom they allow into their breeding rooms. Disease can easily be introduced on the clothing or skin of visitors. If in doubt, keep them out!

11. If you suspect that one of your rabbits is ill, do not lose any time in isolating it. This is obviously crucial if a number of rabbits are owned.

EXERCISE

All rabbits should have ample time to exercise. Even a large cage or hutch cannot provide the room needed for this activity. If you are unprepared or unable to provide your rabbits with adequate time out of the cage, the hard reality is that you should not keep rabbits as pets. Sadly, this fact is ignored time and again, and nothing is more sad than to see a rabbit doomed to a life locked up in a small cage and to be allowed out only infrequently. In this respect, it must be said that breeders are generally the worst offenders. A dog or horse breeder would never dream of setting up kennels or stables without ample exercise paddocks, yet rabbit breeders do just this.

Strangely enough, breeders of long ago were more aware of

Jersey Wooly grooming itself. When grooming, rabbits use their paws much like washclothes.

A lovely Netherland Dwarf rabbit photographed during a break at a rabbit show.

the need to give rabbits ample exercise than are many of today's breeders. The better breeders of yesteryear used to erect brick hutches, each with an enclosed walled run attached to it. Smaller units were made of wood and had chicken-wire runs. Large Morant hutches were commonplace so that the rabbits could be given time in the fresh air and could graze on grass. It seems that today the emphasis has largely changed to one of keeping rabbits under intensive farm-like conditions. This results in high standards of hygiene, but the general consideration of a rabbit's need to run around is the tradeoff. In reality, this doesn't need to be the case.

Breeding Dwarf Rabbits

Before you attempt to get underway in a breeding program, you should first sit back and consider the situation very carefully. There is no benefit whatsoever in breeding for its own sake: it will prove a costly undertaking of which you will quickly tire. The reproduction of any animal species must therefore have a very definite objective. In fancy breeds of rabbit, there are essentially two types of breeder. One is basically in the hobby for no other reason than to make money from it. The other is the person who wishes to produce good stock that can

be exhibited or sold as exhibition quality. Such breeders simply love breeding rabbits. If a few dollars can be made in doing so, there is nothing wrong with this.

The first type of breeder tries to cut every possible corner so that his overhead is minimal, yet he will try to get top dollar for stock that is invariably mediocre to rubbish. Such breeders are the scourge of all animal hobbies. They move from one pet or breed to another as a pet or breed becomes popular and for which demand often exceeds supply. Needless to say, dwarf rabbits have such

If you are interested in starting a breeding program, you should first establish whether you really have the time necessary for such an endeavor. Rabbits require regular daily care and will not thrive if they do not receive it.

Acquiring quality stock and establishing yourself as a reputable breeder in the show world can be costly. Rabbit breeding should not be looked upon as a money-making venture.

Specimens in any given litter can range from excellent to just average.

breeders because this group of rabbits is gaining tremendous popularity; and quality stock is not actually available in an overflow and is not ever likely to be.

THE PITFALLS OF BREEDING

If you plan to be a reputable breeder, this will mean that your objectives are to steadily improve your stock by applying good judgment and making shrewd purchases. Your stock will be housed under the best possible conditions, and it will be fed to the same high standards. You will become a member of your national rabbit organization and will register your best stock. All of this will cost you a lot of time and money, against which there are no guarantees that you will be successful.

The first problem that you will encounter is that in any one litter of bunnies there may be not a single individual that will meet exhibition standards. Even when you are well established, this does not mean that most of your litters could be regarded as quality offspring. Indeed, the majority will not be. They will range from excellent to average, the latter being sound representatives of the breed that will make nice pets. Gaining recognition as a good breeder is costly in itself. You will need to have your stock exhibited on a regular basis, and this is costly and time consuming. If you eventually make it to the top and cared to add up your annual overhead—even allowing for a few big-dollar sales of stock—you will be unlikely to cover your costs. So, from the outset, accept that rabbit breeding is not a money-making hobby. You must therefore be able to support your program from your present income, maybe defraying part of the cost with the sale of surplus stock produced.

INITIAL CONSIDERATIONS

The very first thing you must do in planning to breed rabbits is to find out if this is even permissible in your locality. In urban settings, there may be ordinances that forbid the breeding of any livestock, or such activities may be restricted in the number of pets that can be bred in any one dwelling. There may be regulations regarding the type of building that is utilized, and neighbors may need to be consulted first.

Assuming there are no legal problems, your next consideration is whether or not you really do have the time, space, and cash to conduct even a small program. The biggest problem beginners have to overcome is their impatience to get underway. Often they will hammer some galvanized wire mesh onto packing cases, rush out and purchase whatever stock is available (preferably in kindle does), and sit back and

call themselves breeders!

Regard your breeding operation as you would a business. Plan all details carefully—this is actually half the fun. By the time you have estimated all costs, you may change your mind about the idea of being a breeder; thus, a prudent approach to matters could save you long-term time and cash. Do not compromise on the quality of either accommodations or initial stock. If your budget is tight, then start in a very small way, or maybe concentrate on preparing the accommodations the first year and starting up your program the following year. The latter course of action gives you valuable time to seek out just the stock that you really want.

Above: Before starting a breeding program, you should check with your local municipality regarding the legality of such a practice. **Left:** Dwarf rabbits are notably small animals, but breeding them will still require ample space if they are to be housed comfortably—as they should be.

Jersey Woolies. Small rabbit breeds mature much sooner than the larger rabbit breeds.

is also true of more than a few long-time breeders).

1. All that glitters is not gold. Never assume that a top-winning rabbit

Mini Lop.

BREEDING THEORY

Your success as a breeder will be determined by whether or not you can apply the basic principles of genetics to your breeding program. It is therefore worthwhile that you take time out to study at least the fundamentals of heredity. They are rather important if you have any inclination to specialize in given color varieties and could save you a lot of wasted matings. Here I will relate a few aspects of genetics that beginners often do not appreciate (a fact that

is automatically a good breeding animal. A superb rabbit can be the result of very careful breeding, but it can also be the result of pure chance in the way its genes have been inherited. It may never produce a rabbit of any merit at all. A winning rabbit is determined by its external appearance alone, not by how, from a genetic viewpoint, that appearance was gained.

This being so, you should purchase your initial stock from a very reputable breeder who has a good track record

Jersey Woolies. Understanding the basics of genetics will be very helpful in your breeding program endeavors.

of consistently producing winning stock. The chances are strong that he has utilized very careful breeding practices and not relied on hit-or-miss methods (which can *sometimes* produce some outstanding winners). You want to know that the rabbits that you purchase not only have visual virtues but also good characteristics that they will pass on to their offspring.

2. Understand breeding strategies. Do your homework so that you fully understand the differences between inbreeding (of which line breeding is a dilute form), outcrossing, like-to-like matings, unlike-to-unlike matings, and the consequences of all of these combinations. For example, it is often stated that close inbreeding always results in greater homozygosity—in other words, "purer" stock. In itself, this

statement is incorrect, as is the statement that close inbreeding creates problems.

Inbreeding may actually increase the variation in a given stock and thus increase heterozygosity unless it is accompanied by rigid selection. The matter of selection is therefore absolutely crucial to breeding success; otherwise, the best stock in the world will steadily deteriorate with successive generations—a fact that those with unlimited cash do not always seem to appreciate. You

Mini Rexes. Random selections for breeding may produce noteworthy rabbits, but in most cases this is simply a matter of good luck.

Netherland Dwarf.

Head Study of a Netherland Dwarf. Note the bold, bright eyes, which are desirable in this breed.

Netherland
Dwarf,
smoke
pearl.

level. Both sexes pass exactly half of their genes to their offspring, so one parent has no more influence than the other on the individuals that they produce. It is a joint affair. However, in breeding programs, the buck is more important than the doe in one vital respect: he is able to transfer his genes (thus virtues or faults) through a given population at a vastly more rapid rate than can a doe. Does are limited to a certain number of litters in a year. The buck can sire literally hundreds of litters over the same period. The choice of a suitable buck for your own stud is thus a matter of great importance. You should therefore be prepared to pay a good price for a proven male if you wish to use him repeatedly in your breeding program.

cannot buy success, only quality stock. Thereafter, selection methods—not just genetics—will determine success.

Inbreeding raises the potential for bringing faults to the fore; it does not create them (unless it is continued well beyond the level that the average breeder is ever likely to practice). If a given fault is not within your stock, no amount of inbreeding will introduce it.

3. The buck is more important than the doe (or vice versa). You may hear this statement many times; but it is totally untrue, at least at the individual litter

4. Purchase your initial stock from the same breeder.

This is wise advice, but it can be modified a little if you wish. The benefits of having a trio (or more) of rabbits from a single breeder of repute is that you commence with known gene (blood) lines. If you purchase a doe from one breeder and a buck from another, you could undue, in the first generation, all the years of work both breeders have put into their stock. However, there can be merit in obtaining a buck and doe from one breeder and a related (distant) doe from another breeder. By doing so, you can develop two lines of stock that have a common buck and a distant line relationship that could prove a useful outcross if it was needed. In other words, all your eggs are not in one basket but in two similar baskets. This gives you flexibility to continue with a proven line while seeing how a second line fares using the same buck. With such a breeding platform, it is possible to conduct a closed program for quite a few generations. This means breeding without the need to introduce outside bloodlines and maybe genes of unknown status. Very often, a novice breeder will mix breeding lines without ever having really persevered with what he already has in terms of his stock's virtues. From the few aspects discussed, you can appreciate that burying your head in a breeding-theory book, instead of a thriller, can be of really practical benefit to you from the outset.

A final comment on preplanning is that you are advised to initially keep things on a low-key level. The last thing that you need to happen is to be overrun with offspring at a time when you have little practical experience. In this situation, you could find that you have more babies than you can

Polish. When starting your breeding program, keep it on a low-key level: don't overstock, or you may wind up with an over-abundance of youngsters—which may be more than you can handle.

The age at which sexual maturity occurs can vary from breed to breed. Although dwarf rabbit does reach sexual maturity at the age of about 3½-months, it is better to breed them after they have reached the age of 6 months.

dispose of easily. Start with perhaps two does, at the most three. Let your new hobby develop slowly if you find that you are as happy with it as you had originally hoped. You may find that you need to upgrade your breeding stock, which is much more difficult if you have committed all your funds and space from the word go.

weeks, but it is best to wait until she is more physically mature before expecting her to bear and raise a litter. This being so, she can be bred anytime after she is six months old. A maiden doe is best mated to an experienced buck and vice versa. Your young female(s) should be paired to well-proven bucks of quality. Never breed your

BREEDING FACTS AND PROCEDURES

By preparing for a breeding program in a planned way, you are much less likely to run into problems and will not be unduly surprised by them when they occur. Now let us look at practical aspects of breeding.

Breeding Age

Your dwarf rabbit doe may be sexually mature anytime after the age of about 14

females excessively. Four litters a year would be a reasonable maximum that allow the doe to recoup her physical condition between each pregnancy. Three might be better. You are not in the commercial rabbit-production business and so do not need to adopt commercial strategies, which are for a very different objective.

Breeding Cycle

Rabbits, unlike cats and

dogs, do not have an obvious estrus cycle. They are termed induced ovulators. This means that the presence of a male is sufficient for them to come into breeding readiness. In actual fact, they do cycle about every 13 to 14 days out of every 16, which is why a cycle is hardly evident. You can tell whether or not your doe is likely to be receptive to a buck by inspecting her vulva. The color of it ranges from white to pink to purple. The purple color indicates sexual readiness and will be accompanied by a slight liquid discharge from the vulva.

Mating Procedure

The doe is *always* taken to the cage or hutch of the buck. If after a few minutes of being chased she shows aggression toward her suitor, then she is not ready for mating. Try her the next day and so on until she is prepared to be mounted. Once a mating is observed, she can be removed; and a repeat mating can be undertaken about 12 hours later. This will normally

Jersey Wooly. An element of chance exists in virtually all breeding programs, but this uncertainty offers a challenge and excitement to most breeders.

Selection for breeding is not an easy matter. It requires the breeder's careful attention if the quality of a given strain is to be consistently maintained.

Netherland
Dwarf,
Siamese
smoke pearl.

maximize the litter size. Do not leave her with the buck after a mating. Otherwise, he will simply continue to chase and mate her, and she will become stressed.

Pregnancy Detection

Although abdominal swelling about three weeks after breeding might indicate a pregnant doe, this is not a reliable guide—she may simply be getting fat! Likewise, test matings after a couple of weeks are not conclusive either way. They can create birth problems in a pregnant doe, which may develop a second "round"of fetuses resulting from the test mating.Palpation is the only sure method of pregnancy determination. It can be performed any time after about the tenth to twelfth day following the mating. Carefully feel the abdomen when the tiny fetuses, which are round and pea sized, can be felt. They grow rapidly after this time, and they get softer to the touch as well. Feel the doe's mid-belly area about the level of her hind legs.

You are unlikely to harm the fetuses at this age because they are well protected. If you are unsure about the technique, your vet or an experienced breeder can show you how to do it.

Nestbox

Your doe will need to be supplied with a nestbox about two days prior to the anticipated day of birth. It can be supplied earlier than this, but doing so merely encourages the doe to use it as a place to sleep, and she might foul it with fecal matter. The size of the box should reflect the size of the breed. As a guide, it should be just a little longer than the doe when she is in the posed position and a couple of inches wider than her maximum width. It can be made of metal, wood, or plastic. (The last item on this list is a very good choice.) You can drill a few holes in the base of the nestbox so that any excess urine will slowly drain out.Line the box with shredded or granular paper and then put in a generous layer of hay. The doe will shape the nest and give it a final lining with her

Any rabbits that you wish to breed should be in top physical condition. Providing your rabbits with a proper diet can help you to achieve this goal.

own fur. A few dried leaves in her cage may well be appreciated by her. There are many commercial nestboxes from

devoid of hair but appear so as their hair is fine and wet. They develop rapidly: their eyes and ears

which you can choose, but try to avoid using overlarge boxes as is often done by beginners. The doe prefers a cozy nest.

The nestbox should be removed at the latest about 21 days after kindling (birth), somewhat earlier in warmer weather. It must be well sanitized before it is used again. After a good cleaning, it can be left in a sunny location as pathogens do not survive well in direct sunlight.

Gestation Period

This is the time between the fertilization of an egg and the actual birth of the babies. In rabbits, it is 30 to 33 days. If a litter is not produced by the 33rd day, contact your vet, who can induce parturition. If this is not done, it is possible that the litter will be stillborn (dead at birth).

Development

Rabbits are born blind and quite helpless. They are not

are open by about the 10th day, and by 17th day they will be scrambling about out of the nest.

Litter Size

This obviously can vary with the individual breed and doe, but the range in dwarf rabbits would be one to eight. (This range is smaller than that for the larger rabbit breeds, as might be expected.) A typical dwarf litter would perhaps be four to five in number. Mortality of offspring early in life will vary from breed to breed and from doe to doe. It is very much influenced by breeder care (or lack of it). Expect to lose maybe one baby, possibly two in a large litter.

Rearing Youngsters

The offspring will feed totally from their mother for about the first 21 days and thereafter will start to take solid foods. Some youngsters

Jersey Wooly. In rabbits, the gestation period is about 30 to 33 days, but this timeframe can vary somewhat.

will start to eat solid foods at an earlier age.

Weaning

The process of a youngster ceasing to feed from its mother is called weaning. It can occur anytime from four to eight weeks after the birth of the babies. It need not be a rushed procedure. Forced early weaning may have an adverse effect on the subsequent character of a pet rabbit in later life. Once the youngsters are weaned onto solid foods, keep the litter together for at least a few days. Doing so will reduce the potential for stress.

Identification

Presently, there are a few widely used methods to provide identification for a rabbit: tattooing and leg banding. *Check with your national rabbit association regarding its regulations in this matter.*

Record Keeping

Even if you conduct only a small breeding program, you should keep detailed records; and never commit facts to memory. Record the registration numbers of the rabbits that were mated, when the kits were born, how many, their sex, color, birth weight (as well as subsequent periodic weight measurements), and what problems, if any, were encountered, including numbers of any that died. The more detailed that your records are, the more valuable they may be to you at a later date. You can appreciate that breeding is a subject that can fill an entire book and that there are many things that can go wrong during the prenatal and postnatal periods. That which has been discussed here will give you the essential facts, but you should seek more detailed texts before getting underway as a breeder.

Be sure to keep written records for all of the rabbits that you breed. Never rely just on memory.

Exhibition

The exhibition side of the rabbit fancy, while primarily concerned with competitions, does in fact fulfill a number of other important roles. It allows breeders and any other rabbit enthusiasts to meet, socialize, and exchange ideas and experiences. It is the shop window for products, clubs, and all that is new in the hobby, including placing new breeds in front of interested hobbyists. At a show, you can see more breeds and varieties of rabbit than would be possible at any other location.

The show is thus the marketplace for the hobby, and more than in a metaphorical sense, because you can also purchase stock at these events. You can also make contacts for future purchases or sales. All potential rabbit owners should therefore attend one or more exhibitions in order to

Exhibition serves as a showcase for new breeds and color varieties. Some hobbyists find exhibition to be the most exciting aspect of the hobby.

get a sense of the breeds and a flavor of the hobby itself. The ways in which shows in the USA and Britain are organized does differ somewhat, as does the method of making up champions. Here, we are limited by space, and so what follows is a basic overview of the exhibition side of the hobby. If you are interested in becoming an exhibitor, simply attend one or two shows, talk to exhibitors, and you will soon be familiar with the way things are done in your country.

TYPES OF SHOWS

Shows fall into several categories based on whether or not they are cooped (penned) and whether or not

local affair is called a carrying-box show. In this type of show, the exhibitors keep their exhibits in carrying boxes and take them to the judge's table when it is time for their class to be judged. From a spectator viewpoint, the cooped shows are obviously the better ones to visit not only because the rabbits are easily seen but also because they are larger shows as well. Finally, in some shows you will need to enter the show ahead of time; in others, you may enter on the show day. Same-day-entry shows will, again, generally be the smaller, local club exhibitions.

A show may be devoted to a single breed, a group of breeds, or all breeds. A large

Dwarf Hotot. This is a good way to hold a dwarf rabbit. Notice how the front and back legs are firmly secured.

they are for a single breed or many breeds. A cooped show is one in which coops or pens are provided for the exhibits. The alternative, which is typical of the smaller, more

show may span a number of days, while smaller events will be of a single day's duration. Shows are advertised in local and national club newsletters, rabbit magazines, and very

Seal point Holland Lop. This rabbit is a senior doe. Rabbits can be entered into a number of classes based on their breed, age, color, and variety. Show qualifications vary from country to country.

often in the local press or in the windows of pet shops. You can also write to your national rabbit association for information on forthcoming shows in your area.

SHOW CLASSES

Rabbits are entered into the various classes based on their breed, age (also called class), color (variety), and sex. As far as dwarf rabbits go, there are only two age classes: senior and junior. In the USA, a senior buck or doe is one that is six months of age or more on the day of a show; a junior is a rabbit under six months of age. In the UK, the club sponsoring the show will determine age qualifications for young rabbits, either by month, or between months— for example, under five

months of age or five to six months of age.

Classes will be available for each of the recognized colors, and any color that is not presently recognized will be shown in the Any Other Color (AOC) class, providing it is a recognized color pattern in another breed. There are also classes for youth and senior exhibitors. In the USA, a youth is under 19 years of age, in Britain under 16 years of age.

Beyond these basic classes, there will be other classes that are restrictive in one or more ways. For example, in Britain there are novice classes for exhibits that have never won a first.prize other than at a member's table show, a limit class for entries that have not won more than three firsts in open competition, and so on. Finally, there are classes for pets. In these classes, a rabbit need not be of a particular breed, it need not be registered, and it need not carry identification marks. The class may be for the prettiest rabbit, the biggest, the smallest, and so on. These classes encourage many pet owners, especially children, to compete. A number of these participants go on to become serious enthusiasts.

JUDGING

Rabbits are judged on a comparative basis, which means that the judge compares one rabbit to another. There is a fixed number of points allocated to various features of the rabbit. These points indicate the importance of a given feature, be it the fur, the conformation, the color, and so on. This system is somewhat different to that used for many other pets whereby the judge compares each exhibit with a theoretical ideal and deducts points accordingly. Thus, the winner is the rabbit losing the least number of points.

PRIZES

Winning rabbits in each class go on to compete against

other class winners, by variety, sex, and, eventually, breed. Finally, a best-in-show and best-opposite-sex can be declared for that show. The prizes will range from certificates to cups. Of course, in championship shows the rabbits will gain valuable points or a challenge certificate—depending on the country—that will go toward the title of champion.

A Netherland Dwarf bearing identification (an ear tattoo) as required in the USA. In the UK, rabbit identification consists of a leg band.

IDENTIFICATION

In order to compete in a show, a rabbit must carry a permanent form of identification. In the USA, it is a tattoo in the left ear; in the UK, it is a closed leg band that can only be fitted when the rabbit is a few days old.

For British readers, the leg bands are sold by size, and it is vital that the correct size be used. These sizes are: Polish = A, Dwarf Lop and Mini Rex = B, Netherland Dwarf = X. The rings are available from the British Rabbit Council, breed clubs, or approved specialist suppliers. They are year dated.

For American readers, the tattoo can be made with special pliers, with a hand needle, or with an electric needle. These items are available from specialty rabbit outfitters. The actual numbers or letters are left to the breeder to work out. They will normally give an indication of the rabbit's sex, age, variety, and maybe even its sire and dam. A potential breeder/exhibitor is advised to seek instruction from a fellow breeder before performing this procedure for the first time.

THE EXHIBITION RABBIT

The essentials of a show rabbit are that it is very healthy, is at least reasonably representative of its breed, and that it has received basic training in being handled and posed on a table. Any rabbit that arrives at a show in poor health will be eliminated. In such a situation, the problem is not regarded as permanent; and the rabbit in question can enter future shows, assuming its condition is improved. A rabbit arriving at a show with an obvious defect that will not improve with correct care will be disqualified, meaning it cannot enter future shows.

It is most important that a rabbit is handled regularly so that it shows itself to its best advantage when being judged. No matter how good its quality, this may not be evident if the rabbit is wriggling, trying to jump from the table, or attempting to bite the judge! Each breed has its own particular show stance, and the exhibitor should train his rabbits to take up the appropriate pose.

Good physical condition can be achieved only with diligent, continuous attention to nutrition and general husbandry. You cannot bring a rabbit into show condition within a matter of weeks: it must be a year-round occupation.

The exhibition life of a rabbit is limited for a very practical reason. Once a doe commences breeding, she will lose her exhibition

A Polish as it appears in the UK. In the US, this rabbit is known as the Britannia Petite and comes in white only. (The US also has its own breed of Polish.)

Dwarf Hotots. On average, the exhibition life of a dwarf rabbit spans between 1½- to 2½-years of age.

qualities. She will often pull fur from her coat to line her nest. The physical drain on her body as a result of carrying and nursing her offspring will obviously show itself in her appearance when compared to a non-breeding rabbit in peak condition. Likewise, an actively breeding buck, while not so badly affected, will nonetheless not have quite the condition he would have if he were not being bred.

As a rule-of-thumb guide, the upper range for the exhibition life of a dwarf rabbit would be on the order of 18 to 30 months of age. Much beyond 30 months of age, even a very good example would not have quite the edge

it did as a younger exhibit. Given this aspect of showing, you can appreciate that this area of the hobby is the forte of breeders, who have a steady flow of young stock coming through each year.

THE EXHIBITOR

Although you would think that all exhibitors are very fair, caring rabbit owners, the sad truth is that this is not so. There are always those people to whom winning is everything and who will go to any extremes in order to increase their chances of so doing. They will try to dye coat hairs, or they will falsify data such as the rabbit's weight or age. These actions, however, do not affect the good health of the rabbit, whereas those people who deliberately underfeed and even semi-starve their stock in an attempt to keep it within the breed's upper-limit weight can only be regarded as the kind of people that no animal hobby needs within its ranks.

Such mentality merely indicates the exhibitor's total lack of knowledge about rabbits. The size of a rabbit is controlled by gene action. Therefore, no amount of starving will alter its potential but will only make it an obviously skinny and stunted animal. Underfeeding a rabbit may enable it to meet weight requirements; but if it is oversized, this will mean that the rabbit lacks substance. Therefore, underfeeding really is a dead-end policy. A leading judge recently disqualified an exhibit on sight. It was blatantly obvious that the rabbit was undernourished yet barely made the lower weight limit. If it was fed correctly to give it the needed substance that was lacking, it would clearly go beyond the upper limit and so could not qualify as a representative of its breed! Once a breeder is known to employ dubious methods, he rapidly loses all of the respect of his fellows and never achieves any success of note.

It is always nice to win or get in the placings; but when this overrides the fundamental good welfare of one's stock, it is time to get out of the hobby. Showing is all about everyone enjoying himself and sharing a common passion for rabbits. If stock is not doing well, the answer is to upgrade it by purchasing better rabbits, not by trying to doctor inadequate exhibits. Doing so implies that a judge can be hoodwinked, which is rarely the case. Fortunately, the vast majority of exhibitors are honest and wish to win on merit in which they can take pride. Their stock will be highly regarded by other breeders and exhibitors. As a consequence, it will be much sought after.

Showing your dwarf rabbit should be an enjoyable, fun venture. If your stock is not doing well, you can try to upgrade it by purchasing better rabbits.

Health Care

A rabbit getting its claws clipped. When clipping your bunny's nails, take special care to avoid cutting the "quick," or blood vessel, that runs through the nail.

Disease prevention in rabbits and any other livestock is directly related to the conditions under which the rabbits are living. The worse they are the greater the incidence of disease and other health problems. The thrust of the following text is directed at breeders or those who keep a number of rabbits because their rabbits are clearly the ones most at risk. However, the pet owner should be aware of disease prevention and how to cope with problems once they are evident. The text, therefore, also has application to the pet owner.

GENERAL HYGIENE

Always keep on hand a stock of disposable surgical gloves, which should always be used when handling a rabbit that is ill. It is useful to number all feeding utensils and cages so that after cleaning everything is put back in the same place. Never allow any piles of debris or rotting vegetation to accumulate near your rabbitry—doing so is asking for trouble. Once a disease or condition has been identified, general hygiene should be reviewed to try to minimize the spread of the problem or to prevent its recurrence. Very often this is not done effectively, and events simply repeat themselves.

STRESS

There is little doubt that stress is a major player in rabbit problems and disease. Not having visible signs, it is very difficult to pinpoint its cause, but there are certain known situations that will induce it. Overcrowding, fear, noises, transportation, inadequate diet, and undue disturbances all create stress in a rabbit. Clearly, not all rabbits are affected to the same degree, but dwarf breeds are especially prone to stress.

Its effect is to burn up metabolic energy and to make the rabbit's nervous system remain on a state of alert when it should be relaxed.

Eventually, this situation has a negative effect on the immune system, to the degree that it functions poorly. Consequentially, day-to-day minor problems can rapidly become serious and leave the rabbit more open to attack by pathogens than would normally be the case. Overcrowding, cramped quarters, and poor standards of cage cleanliness are conditions that should carefully be prevented as they are proven key areas of stress.

QUARANTINE

Clearly, your rabbit setup cannot be an isolation unit run to laboratory standards of hygiene and security. Nonetheless, you can use such an example to provide a ballpark guide as to an ideal state. Then you can consider how much leeway you have in deviating from such a guide yet have a reasonably acceptable system that will meet your day-to-day needs. The larger the rabbit stud the greater the need to carefully consider what protective

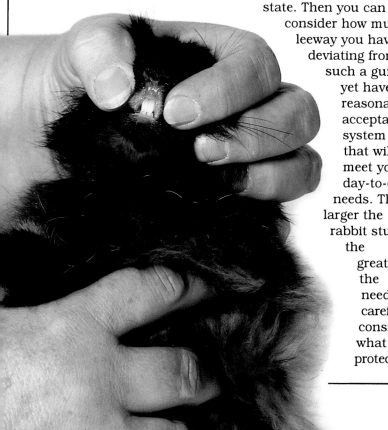

Check your rabbit's teeth on a regular basis. If they become overgrown, your pet will have difficulty eating, which will impact upon the animal's health. (If necessary, your vet can clip your pet's teeth for you.)

Your rabbit's nails should also be checked regularly. If they are allowed to grow too long, this will cause your pet discomfort and impede his mobility.

facility you need. The following are some suggestions. First, there should be separate quarantine and

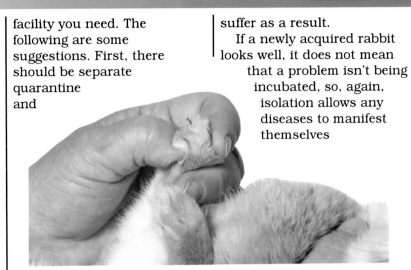

suffer as a result.

If a newly acquired rabbit looks well, it does not mean that a problem isn't being incubated, so, again, isolation allows any diseases to manifest themselves

hospital facilities. There is no benefit in combining these units: it is obviously dangerous to place a quarantined newcomer in the same environment as a rabbit that is known to be ill. Therefore, at least three rooms or buildings are needed for an efficient rabbit stud. One for stock, one for hospitalization, and one for quarantine.

In the matter of quarantine, a minimum isolation period should be 14 days, though 21 would be better. During this period, you can monitor both the health and the feeding of newcomers. Bear in mind that when a rabbit moves from one area to another, it will take with it localized bacteria with which its immune system has become familiar. At the same time, its body will need to become accustomed to local bacteria in its new home. It is therefore better that this is done in isolation rather than placing the rabbit in with the main stock—where both could

away from your main stock. Remember also that if you are a regular exhibitor, your stock is being exposed to health risks at shows. This is a hard reality that is sometimes downgraded. While we would hope that all exhibits are in the peak of health, it would be naive to think that they could not be carrying a pathogen. Additionally, visitors might have diseased or parasitized animals at home and could be carryiny infectious agents on their skin or clothing. (This type of situation wiped out entire catteries in the early years of cat showing, and only the arrival of vaccinations halted it.) I am by no means suggesting that rabbit showing is a risky business but that exhibitors should minimize the risks by keeping their exhibition stock apart from their main stock or breeding stock. In effect, exhibition rabbits should be quarantined after every outing because they are, in fact, new arrivals in the disease-prevention-view of things.

RECOGNIZING ILL HEALTH

The first signs of ill health are often behavioral, but to notice them you must know your rabbits on an individual basis. Maybe one is not eating as heartily as usual or sits crouched in a corner when it normally bounds toward you. It may be drinking a great deal more than usual (although you may not be aware of it if an automatic water system is in use). It may stiffen up when touched. Any behavioral change has a reason, and so it is an amber warning light that should prompt you to place the rabbit in isolation for further observation. Failure to do so merely allows pathogens more time to establish themselves in your breeding room and stock.

Any clinical signs that are obviously abnormal indicate a problem. Even a slight discharge from the eye or diarrhea should prompt you to hospitalize the patient. Never wait to "see how things are tomorrow"; act today. The hospital cage should be very clean and always sanitized after each use. It should be in a warm room because often heat alone can work wonders on minor problems such as colds. An infrared lamp of the dull emitter type is a worthwhile investment for any breeder.

DIAGNOSING THE PROBLEM

You have noted that a rabbit is not acting normally, and it seems disinterested in its food. You have isolated it and must now move to the next stage, which is diagnosing the problem. Let me say straightaway that diagnosis is a very tricky business. You should note the clinical signs and the rabbit's immediate history; then consult your veterinarian.

The problem with home diagnosis is that the clinical signs of literally hundred of diseases are broadly similar. How do you know which one your rabbit has? Even your vet may need to take skin scrapings or conduct microscopy on fecal matter and/or blood samples in order to identify a pathogen. Until the pathogen is identified, it is quite impossible to commence

This unfortunate Netherland Dwarf is suffering from a bacterial infection and a secondary eye infection. Observing the basic rules of good husbandry can lessen the chances of your pet being stricken ill by disease.

treatment. A long-standing breeder, through practical experience of having encountered certain conditions and diseases, may be able to identify them; but then again, he could be wrong.

The beginner should document all signs and then discuss them with the vet, rather than refer to a text on diseases and assume the

is useful to have a first-aid chest at a convenient location. Items in it should include: bandages, cotton swabs, curved scissors, a styptic pencil (to treat small cuts), antiseptic and antibiotic lotions or ointments, nail clippers, eye lotion, iodine (useful for treating ringworm, a fungal infection), veterinary-recommended treatments for fleas and other parasites, and

Netherland Dwarfs. Your vet is the person best qualified to diagnose a health problem in your rabbit. If your pet is ill, a trip to the vet is in order; don't rely on medical texts and try to make a diagnosis yourself.

descriptions match the clinical signs exhibited by his rabbit. In any case, most of the modern drugs for treating rabbit diseases—and diseases of other animals as well—are obtainable only from a veterinarian.

THE FIRST-AID CHEST
In order to be prepared to cope with minor problems, it

a veterinary-recommended emulsion for mild stomach upsets.

HEAT STROKE AND SHOCK
In the event that a rabbit is suffering from heat stroke, which is indicated when the rabbit is prostrate and panting, the first thing to do is to bring down its body temperature. Carefully

immerse the animal in a tub of tepid water, holding its head well above the water's surface. Wipe the head with a wet towel. After a few minutes the rabbit should be placed in a cool, dry, shady area until complete recovery is effected.

If your pet is ever badly frightened by a dog, cat, or other cause, it may go into shock—this may happen some minutes after the initial fright. Put the rabbit in a warm, quiet, and darkened room so that it can recover. In the event that it has been bitten, it should be wrapped in a towel and taken straight to your vet for treatment of the wound and the accompanying shock.

NAIL TRIMMING

You should inspect the nails of your pets on a regular basis. If they grow too long, they can easily be trimmed with dog pliers or those of the guillotine type, which are actually better. What you must avoid is trimming the "quick," or blood vessel, in the nail. It is easily seen in flesh-colored nails but not in black nails or those of other dark colors. Have an assistant hold the bunny on its back and carefully trim a little at a time. With a dark nail, a pencil flashlight should enable you to see the blood vessel. It is better to cut off too little than risk hurting your pet.

RABBIT DISEASES

Rabbits can suffer from the same extensive range of diseases as can other animals, including us humans. These diseases have not been discussed in this chapter because the limitations of space would have made doing so futile and unproductive. Your first line of defense is always preventive husbandry. If you wish to advance your knowledge of diseases, you are advised to invest in a larger volume about rabbits or one that is devoted to diseases of small mammals. Your objective in such a study should not be in order to try and diagnose or treat your stock but to have a better understanding of the life cycle of given pathogens and thus how you can combat these pathogens with preventive techniques.

For example, you may not be aware that certain disinfectants may have no value in killing given pathogens or that using given chemicals in double or more concentrated doses does not increase their efficacy. This kind of knowledge can have far more practical value to you than attempting diagnosis and treatment of diseases—for which only a veterinarian is trained and has the facilities and medicines to attend to.

The Dwarf Breeds

As with all but the more recent breeds, the origin of dwarf rabbits is undocumented. The earliest records seem to date back to about the 1850s, when the name Polish was applied to small red-eyed white rabbits that were in existence in Britain. The name thus has no known associations with the country of Poland, a fact that is also true of many other pets that bear the names of countries with which they have no association. It is probably from the English Polish that the present genes for dwarfism have spread to the other diminutive breeds.

The original dwarf rabbits, as mentioned in the introduction, were plagued with problems. This situation certainly restricted their popularity for many years—much in the same way that the present-day gorgeous rex breeds were originally regarded as wrecks or ugly freaks when they were first produced. I recall vividly a neighbor friend of mine in England who bred Polish and Netherland Dwarfs in the 1950s. He was convinced that he would make a fortune with these diminutive bunnies. Eventually, he gave them up in favor of Dutch and English because of a series of disasters that seemed to accompany most dwarf litters.

In those days, malocclusion of the teeth was a real problem, as was lack of fertility and extreme nervousness. Sometimes youngsters would literally die of fright if they were startled into panicky dashes around the hutch. They also seemed to suffer from lack of resistance to most ailments. So, one way or another, it took a very special type of breeder to persist with dwarf rabbits and weed out all sickly stock.

Opposite page: Netherland Dwarf. Early on in their history, dwarf rabbits were beset with a number of problems including infertility, extreme nervousness, and malocclusion. Fortunately, this is no longer the case.

Netherland Dwarf. The history of the original dwarf rabbits is not known for certain.

The problem was that there were many breeders who felt they would make good profits from the Polish and the Netherland Dwarfs. By interchanging the small gene pools of stock, many merely perpetuated the existing problems. However, slowly but steadily the dedicated breeders concentrated on producing fine healthy examples, and the bad reputation the dwarfs had gained started to recede to a very large extent.

Once the Polish and Netherland Dwarfs had overcome their early development of new varieties of dwarf rabbit.

It is a certainty that the present dwarfs, as a group, will attract an evergrowing number of followers in the coming years. These numbers will be swelled by the development of more new-dwarf breeds. However, as this happens, there is always the risk that the clock will be turned back. Indiscriminate breeders, in an effort to make quick money, will produce sickly examples. It must always be remembered that while most of the past problems with dwarfs are no

The Netherland Dwarf has been instrumental in the development of several other dwarf-type rabbits.

problems, they became strong favorites on the show bench, especially the Netherland. It was clear that it would not be too long before breeders attempted to transfer the dwarf gene to other breeds; and we are now seeing, especially in the USA, greater efforts being placed into the longer major issues, this is not to suggest that the genes that caused those problems years ago are no longer present. Only by the judicious selection of the finest youngsters for breeding stock can past problems be kept to a low level of incidence.

In the following breed

descriptions, the dwarf rabbits are presented in order of length of establishment—the oldest first. These breed descriptions are of a general nature. Those who require more specific details are referred to the appropriate national standards: those of the American Rabbit Breeders Association (ARBA) or those of the British Rabbit Council. The list of faults given for each of the breeds is by no means complete but serves to draw attention to those faults that are especially important. In exhibition stock, these faults are either penalized or sufficient to justify disqualification.

THE POLISH (UK) OR BRITANNIA PETITE (USA)

The breed known as the Polish in Britain is somewhat different from that known by the same name in the USA. Originally, this situation created a great deal of confusion, but eventually the Americans overcame it by using the name Britannia Petite to apply to the British Polish. As discussed earlier in this chapter, the Polish is generally held to be the

original dwarf and was exhibited in Hull, Yorkshire as long ago as 1884. In Britain, it is a popular breed, no doubt

The Polish as seen in the UK. This breed is sprightly and full of spirit. When exhibited, it stands high up on its front legs and holds its head proudly.

in part because it is seen in many colors. In the USA, its counterpart is an albino and is relatively rare—with annual registrations not even reaching double figures in some years.

Brief Description

This is a diminutive, fine-boned, and compact breed that has a maximum acceptable weight of 2.5 lbs. (1.1kg), although the ideal weight is 2 lbs. (0.79kg). This makes the Polish, along with

Netherland Dwarf. This breed has the distinction of being the most popular show rabbit in the US and also has a large following in the UK and Europe.

the Netherland Dwarf, the smallest rabbit breed in the world. The fur is short and fine with a sleek sheen to it. It is termed *fly back*, which means that it will return instantly to its normal lie when stroked from rump to shoulders. The head is pleasingly wedge-shaped in profile but with a soft rounded contour. The abdomen is well tucked up, the show stance being termed a full arch. The breed should always present the impression of being highly alert, standing well up on

its front feet when being exhibited.

The ears are short, well furred, and should touch all the way up without displaying a flat surface or flange. They are longer than those of the Netherland Dwarf but must not exceed 2.5 in. (6.3cm). The eyes are round and bold. The latter term does not mean bulging but rather that they

are prominent when compared to those of most other rabbit breeds. The legs are slender and graceful, never too short or never giving the impression of being heavily boned.

Colors

In the USA, the only recognized color is white with ruby red eyes. In Britain, many colors are accepted, as is the blue-eyed white. These colors are divided into the following groups: Selfs, Shaded Selfs, Agouti Pattern, Tan Pattern, Other Varieties, and Marked.

Faults

Any tendency toward overlength in the body or cobbiness. Sparse coats, those that are overlong or that feature long guard hairs, or roll back fur. Odd-colored eyes, pale eyes, wall eyes. White patches on colored rabbits and white toenails on anything other than red- or blue-eyed whites.

NETHERLAND DWARF

This lively little breed is thought to have been developed in mainland Europe from crossings based on the British Polish breed, which was exported to Germany, Holland, and other countries, possibly about the 1870s. It is said that the Polish was

crossed with the Dutch in Germany to produce the breed known as the Hermelin. However, things must be put into perspective when looking back to the 19th century because at that time the Dutch itself was not an established breed. Another theory is that the Polish (or Pol[e], as it is known in Holland) was crossed with a small wild rabbit, and from this mating the dwarf was developed.

Certainly, it was not until the early 20th century that an established type became evident. The breed arrived in England about 1948. It may be that examples of these early mainland-Europe dwarfs reached England from Holland, and this would account for the name *Netherland Dwarf*. To this day,

there is controversy over the true lineage of the breed, and it is doubtful if it will ever be known for sure.

Be this as it may, the breed proved highly successful but did suffer the same problems as its Polish ancestor. By the late 1950s, it was becoming an extremely well-established British favorite but, perhaps surprisingly, did not gain status in the USA until 1969. It initially created all kinds of problems for the Americans who often crossed it with the two Polish breeds. The situation was eventually resolved when the British Polish was renamed the Britannia Petite, and the Netherland Dwarf and the American Polish become identifiable distinct breeds.

Today, the Netherland Dwarf is easily America's most

A pair of Himalayan Netherland Dwarfs. The Netherland Dwarf is the smallest breed of rabbit in the world.

popular show rabbit and is hardly less popular in Britain and mainland Europe, where it is known as the European Pole. Its popularity is well justified because it is an extremely cute little bunny that wins devotees the minute they first see it. It is available in just about every color and pattern combination and so is a great favorite with those who specialize in color breeding. This is the best way to proceed from a breeding viewpoint because it enables the breeder to concentrate on quality, rather than try to spread his efforts across too many colors.

Brief Description

The Netherland is superficially very similar in appearance to the Polish, but there are some important differences that can be noted once you become familiar with these breeds. The Netherland is a more compact and cobby rabbit. When posed, it shows no light under its abdomen and does not stand erect on its front feet. The head in profile is altogether more rounded, especially in the arc from the ears to the nose. The male's head is larger than that of the female. The ears are shorter than those of the Polish, being no more than 2 in. (5cm) in length. They must be well furred but may not necessarily touch each other as in the Polish. The eyes are round and bold. The coat is short, dense, glossy, and of the roll back type. This means that it does not fly back to its original position when stroked against its lie but instead returns more gradually. The Netherland has the same upper-weight limit as the Polish (UK) and Britannia Petite (USA): 2.5 lbs. (1.1kg), although the ideal specimen will be about 2.2 lbs. (1kg).This breed is seen in all colors. For show purposes, it is divided into groups. While it has less groups than the British Polish, there are nonetheless more varieties to select from within its groups. Among those that are additional to those seen in the British Polish are the following: Seal Point Siamese and Otter. The Netherland groups also include a number of shades not presently available in the British Polish. Both red- and blue-eyed whites are seen in this breed. In the colored varieties, the eye color may be gray or brown, according to the variety.

Faults

Lack of width in the shoulders, poor ear carriage or excess ear length, narrow non-rounded face, white toenails in colored rabbits, fly back coat, sparse coat, wall eyes, excess weight, possession of a dewlap, , pointed or Roman nose, white hairs in a self-colored coat, and incorrect teeth alignment. There are also colored-related faults within each of the varieties.

POLISH (AMERICAN)

The breed known as the Polish in the USA may be likened to a large Netherland Dwarf rather than to the British Polish. Its origins are obscure but no doubt originate from the British Polish. There may well have been an infusion of other small-breed genes into this breed, for it is known that albino Dutch and other diminutive albinos were shown and bred as being Polish. Most certainly, the Netherland Dwarf figures in its ancestry as well. This is evident in the American Polish's appearance.

Unlike the Britannia Petite, the American Polish is seen in a number of colors, and this no doubt accounts for the fact that it is far more popular than the Petite.

breed with an upper-limit acceptable weight of 3.5 lbs. (1.6kg), though the ideal would be 2.5 lbs. (1.1kg)—the maximum weight of the British Polish and the Netherland Dwarf.The ears of the Polish are longer than those of the Netherland, having an acceptable length of up to 3 in. (7.6cm). As in the British Polish, the ears should touch each other along their length and display no flat surface where they meet. The neck is short, which is standard for all dwarf breeds.

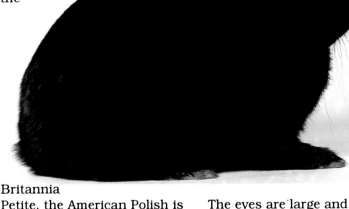

The Polish (as seen in the US). This breed is small and compact with an ideal weight of 2½ lbs.

Brief Description

The general shape of the American Polish is comparable to the Netherland Dwarf but with a few differences of note. For one thing, the Polish is a larger

The eyes are large and round. The fur is short, dense, sleek, and of the fly back type.

The present colors are as follows: Black with brown eyes; blue with blue-gray eyes; chocolate with brown eyes; white with either ruby or blue eyes.

Faults

Excess body length, dewlap, pointed nose, incorrect head

shape, colored toenails on a white specimen, white toenails on a colored specimen, poor white, white hairs in a colored variety.

today. The Dwarf Lop derived from the same breeder that bred the Holland: the Dutchman Adrian De Cock. It may well be that some of the early British stocks were

Mini Lop. In general appearance, the Mini Lop is thickset and heavily muscled. It sports a thick, lustrous coat.

MINI, HOLLAND, AND BRITISH DWARF LOPS

These three breeds are superficially very similar in many respects. (The Holland and Mini Lops are not recognized in Britain.) Each of them is a dwarf version of the much larger lops, of which there are four breeds. The oldest is the English, then there is the French, then the Meissner (of Germany), and finally the German Lop. The ancestry of the Dwarf and Holland Lops certainly includes both the English and French Lops and may also include others. However, the tiny lops that we see today are best regarded as mini French Lops with strong dwarf overtones in respect to their conformation.

Some years ago, it was thought that the Dwarf Lop of Britain was the same breed as the Mini Lop of the USA (Meg Brown 1978); but even if this was so originally, it is not so

exported to the USA and became loosely termed Mini Lops. However, the Mini Lop of today was derived from German stock of a breed known in Germany as Kleine Widder. (There is also a lop breed in Germany that is smaller than the Kleine Widder.) Mr. H. Dyke and a Mr. Herschback were the men most prominent in promoting the Mini Lop in the USA. There is little doubt that a variety of breeds have been used in developing the Mini Lop to its present status.

The British Dwarf Lop, in terms of its lineage, has much more in common with the Holland Lop of the USA than with the Mini, but it can be regarded as a totally separate breed. Its weight and conformation will attest to this fact. The Dwarf Lop appears to have first reached Britain from Holland around the mid-1960s. It became an established breed during the following decade. Adrian De Cock conceived the idea of a dwarf French Lop around 1949; but his initial attempts, using dwarf rabbits and French Lops, proved unproductive, or apparently so. An English Lop was then used in the program, and this addition eventually resulted in success. The Mini Lop was accepted as a breed after its showing at the Seattle convention of 1982.

The Holland Lop, the smallest of this trio, first arrived in the USA in 1976. It was given breed status at the Tucson convention of 1979. Since then, the judicious use of dwarfs in its development has resulted in the breed that you see today.

Brief Description

Given that the Mini, Dwarf, and Holland Lops are similar, a single description will serve the purposes of this book, with comments made on specific differences. Potential breeders and exhibitors should refer to the individual standards for the exact wording of the appropriate British and American standards.The upper-weight limit of the British Dwarf Lop is 5.25 lbs. (2.4kg); that of the Mini Lop of the USA is 6.5 lbs.

Netherland Dwarf, Siamese smoke pearl.

Holland Lop, broken fawn. This specimen is a senior buck.

(2.9kg). The Holland Lop is the lightest at 4 lbs. (1.8kg). In all three of these breeds, the impression is of a cobby, thickset rabbit of muscular build. The shoulders are broad, and the chest is deep. The legs are short and thick. The head is more well developed in bucks than in does but should not be narrow or lacking in substance in the female. There is a smooth curve from the crown to the nose when the rabbit is seen in profile.

The crown itself should appear prominent across the top of the skull—a feature of these breeds and of the parent French Lop. This is especially so of the Holland Lop. The cheeks are full, and the eyes are bold and almost round.

The ears are, of course, a very distinctive feature. They are pendular, commencing from the basal crown, and hang down close to the cheeks. They are broad, thick, well-furred, and rounded at their extremity. The ears are not measured in the Mini and Dwarf Lops but should be pleasingly proportionate to the head size. In the Holland, which has the shortest ears, they are required to terminate between one half and one inch below the jaw when the rabbit is holding its head in the normal position.

The desired fur length of the Holland Lop is 1 in. (2.5cm). In the Mini Lop, it should be of medium length; in the Dwarf of the UK, it is required to be of good length

Dwarf Hotot. The obvious distinguishing feature of this breed is the black eyebands that outline the eyes.

with ample guard hairs. In all cases it is fine, dense, glossy, and of a roll back type. The eye colors of the Mini Lop and the Holland Lop should complement the body color. In the Dwarf Lop of Britain, the standard is more explicit with regard to eye color. In the white, the eye color must be ruby red, blue not being acceptable. In the other color varieties, it must be black, ruby, dark hazel, brown, blue, or gray, according to the specific variety. The colors and patterns seen in these dwarf lops are extensive and include selfs, shaded, broken, pointed white, and ticked.

Faults

Long body, narrow shoulders, poor coat, ears that are not fully pendulate from the basal ridge, ears of poor shape and length, excessive dewlap in does, incorrect eye color, incorrect toenail color, white hairs in colored fur, odd-colored and wall eyes, lack of width between the eyes.

DWARF HOTOT

This delightful little rabbit is instantly recognizable because it is pure white with black rings around its eyes. Although marked the same as its larger cousin, the Hotot (Blanc de Hotot), it is not a miniature of that breed but a mixture of Hotot and dwarf genes. It is presently not recognized in Britain. The Hotot itself was developed by Baroness Bernard in France between 1902 and 1912, at much the same time that the Dutch breeder Ziemer was developing a similar breed, the Husumer, in Holland. (The Husumer, however, had a black tail.) The Dwarf Hotot is of German origin, having been developed simultaneously—using different crosses—in both East and West Germany.

The diminutive size was reached in the mid-1970s by crossings involving a black Netherland Dwarf, red-eyed white rabbits, and Hotots.

Springs convention of 1983. While the larger Hotot is struggling to maintain support in the USA, the Dwarf Hotot is faring better.

Brief Description

The Dwarf Hotot ranks number three in the league of diminutive rabbits, having a

Netherland Dwarf, blue-eyed white.

Interbreeding with dwarfs further stabilized and improved the breed. It reached the USA around 1981, having been imported by a Mr. and Mrs. Forstinger. This is actually only three years after the larger Hotot had been imported into Texas. The breed was given full recognition at the Colorado

maximum acceptable weight of 3.25 lbs. (1.5kg). Ideal examples are about one pound lighter. It is a compact breed with a well-arced body when posed in the seated position. The head is characteristic of the dwarf type: set on a neck that is not visually apparent. There is a smooth curve from the ears to the nose when seen in profile. The ears are short, erect, and may or may not touch. They must be well furred. The maximum permitted length is 3 in. (7.6cm), although a somewhat shorter ear is desired. The fur is short, dense, and must exhibit a good sheen. It is of the roll back type. The eye color is a dark brown, and, of course, the black eye band is of great importance to a quality example. The eye band must form a neat, complete, and even ring around the eye. The toenails should be flesh colored or white. The body color is a pure frosty white.

Faults

An obvious neck, a dewlap, a face lacking good width and muzzle, colored toenails, sparse fur, eyes differing in color from that required, an incomplete eye band, and an eye band in which the

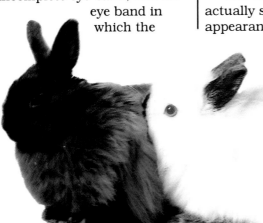

band is irregular in width or features feathering that intrudes on the surrounding white fur.

JERSEY WOOLY

The Jersey is one of the more recent breeds and is named for the state in the USA in which it was developed. It is not recognized in Britain. In appearance, it is dwarf-like in its head features and possesses a profuse coat that is somewhat similar to that seen in the French Angora. It was originated by Bonnie Seeley of High Bridge, New Jersey, during the late 1970s and gained full status at the 1988 convention in Madison, Wisconsin.

A number of breeds— Angoras and other dwarf breeds—were used in its development. The result is a very pleasing little bunny that ranks, along with the American Polish, as the fourth smallest rabbit breed.

Brief Description

The Jersey Wooly is actually smaller than its appearance would suggest. This is because its profuse coat, which should be up to 3 in. (7.6cm) in length, suggests a larger body than really is the case. The upper-weight limit is 3.5 lbs. (1.6kg). The coat is, of

Jersey Woolies. The Jersey, compared to many of the other rabbit breeds, is relatively new on the rabbit scene. Ideal specimens of the Jersey Wooly weigh in at 3 lbs.

course, wooly. Its density and texture are very important attributes of the breed. The coat should be even over the body so that the impression is one of smoothness. The head is typically dwarf, showing a pleasing curve from the crown of the head to the nose. The eyes are large, round, and their color should be appropriate to that of the fur. The ears are short, erect, and may or may not touch along their length. Ear length is about 2.5 in. (6.3cm). Small tufts are acceptable on the ear extremities, but they must never form tassels as seen in the English Angora. The body is short and compact, displaying a nicely arced back when the rabbit is in the posed position.

The feet and legs are neither stocky nor fine boned. They may be wooly, but the front feet should feature normal fur below the first joint. The breed is seen in a wide range of colors and patterns, which are as follows: Agouti, Self, Shaded, Pointed White, and Tan Pattern. In many Jersey Woolies, the relative shortness of the head, feet, and tail fur will mean that these areas are darker than those areas with longer fur.

Faults

An overlong body, lack of depth or well-rounded hips, lack of some fur trimmings on the sides of the head, tassels on the ears, unmatched eye colors, eye color that is not appropriate to that of the fur, fur that is under 1 in. (2.5cm) in length, fur that is uneven over the body, is sparse, or lacks density and good texture.

AMERICAN FUZZY LOP

This is a dwarf lop that sports an Angora-like coat. It is just a little heavier than the Jersey Wooly and, like the Jersey Wooly, displays a larger-than-real size due to its profuse fur. The breed is not recognized in Britain. It was originally developed from crossings between the Holland Lop and the Angora but not with the intent of producing a

American Fuzzy Lop. The heritage of this breed includes Angora-type rabbits as well as the Holland Lop.

new breed: the idea was to improve coat quality in the Holland.

However, as it spread from the West to the East in the USA, breeders noticed that every so often wooly-coated Hollands appeared in litters. The feature was then specifically bred for and stabilized, resulting in the new breed that was accepted at the 1988 Madison, Wisconsin, convention. If you like the Angora coat but prefer a smaller breed, you can thus select from either the flop-eared Fuzzy or the erect-eared Jersey.

Brief Description

The Holland Lop and Angora origins of the American Fuzzy are immediately apparent from the moment you set eyes on a Fuzzy. The massive head, crown, and lop ears of the Holland are as obvious a feature as is the wooly coat of the Angora. The fur should have a length of about 2 in. (5cm) but must never be shorter than 1.5 in. (3.8cm).As in the Holland Lop, the ears should extend one half to one inch below the jaw when it is held in the horizontal position. The Fuzzy is a compact breed showing good width of both shoulders and hips. The body is well filled out and has ample depth. The head is broad and shows good muzzle substance. Side trimmings to the face are accepted. The eyes are round and bold, their color being

Netherland Dwarf, blue-eyed white. This photo clearly illustrates the roundness of the head, which is desirable for the breed.

Mini Rex. Based on appearance only, the Mini Rex gives not the slightest hint of its dwarf heritage. For those who like a velvety rex coat but prefer a smaller rabbit, the Mini Rex is a lovely choice.

ruby, pink, gray, or brown—depending on the fur color.

Color groupings include: Agouti, Broken, Self, Pointed White, Shaded, and Solid, and so they should satisfy the selection needs of all potential devotees.

Faults
Excess body length, lack of substance in the

shoulders, body, or hindquarters. Poor crown ridge, poor fur, be it lack of length, density, or texture (i.e., too silky or fine). Excessive facial trimmings, incorrect eye color, and body colors that are not as required by the color or pattern. Pointed ears or those that are too long, too short, or lack body.

MINI REX
The Mini Rex, which is recognized in both Britain and the USA, is unusual in that it displays no indication of its

dwarf origins. Of course, the major feature of any Rex variety is its stunningly gorgeous velvet-like fur. Add this attractive quality to a diminutive rabbit, and you must end up with a winner from the outset.

The Mini Rex's coat is the result of a mutation that removes the main guard hairs while reducing the size of the secondary guard hairs to that of the underfur, or down, hairs. This mutation has probably appeared numerous times in rabbit history but was first appreciated in France around 1919. However, the early examples could hardly be compared to those of today: their coats were sparse and patchy, and they also suffered from rickets and other health problems. They were introduced into Britain as early as 1926 and gained full recognition in France in 1929. In the years that followed, the Rex not only became a vastly improved breed in terms of its coat but also in respect to its general vigor. Colors were added by crossings with other breeds and then breeding out the other breeds' types.

The development of the Mini Rex in the USA was not a planned happening. Mona Berryhill of Wortham, Texas, discovered a very small rabbit in a litter of normal Rex and sought out a suitable mate for it. A Netherland Dwarf was decided upon. From the resulting offspring, by a careful program, the new breed was created. The breed gained full recognition at the 1988 convention in Madison, Wisconsin. Mona Berryhill remained dedicated to the breed that she created and formed the National Mini Rex Club of America. The Mini Rex's registrations have progressed rapidly over the past several years. It will surely be one of the top breeds in the coming years, possibly even overtaking its larger cousin in numbers exhibited.

Brief Description

Outwardly, the Mini Rex shows no suggestion of its dwarf ancestry and looks a miniature replica of the larger Rex. In Britain, it is judged against the smoothcoated Rex standard, its ideal weight being 3 to 4 lbs. (1.4-1.8kg) and the upper-weight limit being 4.5 lbs. (2.0kg). In the USA, it has its own standard, which is broadly similar to the larger Rex but takes into account the smaller size and the effect it has on fur length and other features. The upper-weight limit in the USA is 4.25 lbs. (1.9kg), but the desired weight is a little lighter than this.The overall impression of the Mini Rex is one of graceful proportions, in which the back line falls in a gentle curve from the hips to the shoulders. It is a well-muscled breed with good shoulder and hip widths. The head sits on a short neck close to the shoulders. In profile, the head is ovoid and does not display the arc that is so characteristic of dwarf rabbits. A small dewlap is permissible in does. The ears are short and erect but not short in comparison to the other dwarfs. They are well covered with fur, carried close together, and display no flat flanges on their inner sides.

The legs and feet are of medium to fine bone, somewhat short in length but always appearing in proportion to the rest of the animal. The eyes are bold and give the appearance of being ovoid in shape. The desired eye color is dependent upon the color of the coat in the various varieties.

The fur of the Rex must be very dense and even so as to give it a plush look and feel. The hair length should ideally be ½ in. (1.28cm). The texture of the hair is required by the British standard to be fine and silky, the springiness being created by the density of hairs. In the USA, fine and silky hairs are regarded as faults, but a lustrous sheen to the hair is required. The apparent difference between

Netherland Dwarfs, orange. This breed comes in a wide variety of beautiful colors.

the two countries' views on texture is more one of interpretation of the words rather than of the actual texture of the fur. It is important that the legs are furred.

The colors available in the Mini Rex are more extensive in Britain than in the USA, but the USA is adding more colors with each year. At this time, the potential colors and patterns are as follows: Self, Shaded, Tan Pattern, Agouti, Dalmatian, Harlequin, Himalayan.

Faults

Excess size and weight, overlong ears, excessive dewlap in does, uneven coat length, lack of density of coat, bare patches of skin on the legs, any tendency to woolliness of the fur, harsh, wavy, crimped or wiry fur, lack of good body to fur causing it to lie flat when stroked, narrow wedge-shaped head, any tendency to appear long or racy in body, incorrect eye color, and any color-related faults, such as white hairs in a solid color.

Useful Addresses

American Rabbit Breeders
Association, Inc.
P.O. Box 426
Bloomington, Illinois 61702
USA

British Rabbit Council
Purefoy House
7 Kirkgate Newark, Notts
NG24 1AD, England

References

T.F.H. Publications offers a comprehensive selection of books dealing with dwarf rabbits and rabbits in general. A selection of significant titles is listed below; they and many other works are available from your local pet shop, booksellers, or T.F.H. Publications itself.

Dwarf Rabbits
by Günther Flauaus
ISBN 0-86622-671-0
TFH H-1073
Hard cover, 5½ x 8", 128 pages, 73 full-color photos

Dwarf Rabbits as a New Pet
by Andrea Dieker and
Jutta Steinkamp
ISBN 0-86622-537-4
TFH TU-026
Soft cover, 6¾ x 8½", 64 pages, 59 full-color photos

Encyclopedia of Pet Rabbits
by D. Robinson
ISBN 0-87666-911-9
TFH H-984
Hard cover, 5½ x 8", 320 pages, 231 full-color photos, 52 black and white photos

Lop Rabbits
by Sandy Crook
ISBN 0-86622-137-9
TFH PS-809
Hard cover, 5½ x 8", 192 pages, 100 full-color photos

The Proper Care of Dwarf Rabbits
by Michael Mettler
ISBN 0-86622-443-2
TFH TW-121
Hard cover, 5 x 7", 256 pages, 100 full-color photos

Index